DA[illegible] THOMPSON

Norman Barrett
Mel Watman

Virgin Books

First published in Great Britain in 1984 by Virgin Books,
61-63 Portobello Road,
London W11 3DD.

Distributed by Arrow Books

Designed and produced by
Autumn Publishing Ltd, 10, Eastgate Square, Chichester
Sussex, England.

Acknowledgements
The competition reports in this book are published by kind permission of *Athletics Weekly*, in which they first appeared. The statistics have been compiled by Alan Lindop. Thanks are also due to *Athletics Weekly* correspondents Dave Cocksedge, Alan Lindop and Brian Smyth for the use of their original reports and extracts from interviews. The authors would also like to acknowledge some quotes used from a Daley Thompson interview with Jon Hendershott for *Track and Field News* (USA).

Picture Credits
All-Sport, Associated Sports Photography, Jorge Lewinski, Mark Shearman, Sportsview, Mike Street.

ISBN 0 86369 0394

Printed in Great Britain by Hazell Watson and Viney Ltd
Designed by Nigel Standerline
Typesetting by Project Reprographics, Chichester

CONTENTS

About the authors

Mel Watman is one of Britain's foremost authors on athletics and has been Editor of *Athletics Weekly* since 1968. He has written and compiled several books on athletics, including *The Encyclopedia of Athletics*.

Norman Barrett, a freelance sports writer, originated and edited the sports weekly part-work *The Game*. He has written and edited a number of books and encyclopedias on sport.

1
INTRODUCTION

Whichever way you look at it, Daley Thompson has to be considered the most successful British athlete of all time. There are other serious candidates for that distinction, from Sydney Wooderson to Sebastian Coe. But none can point to such an imposing array of international honours as Daley, who is still improving and learning and who can, if he keeps healthy and sufficiently motivated, look forward to several more seasons as the world's greatest all-round athlete.

Daley's championship record in decathlon is simply awe-inspiring. He has fought for seven major titles since 1977 and won six of them — the 1977 European Junior, 1978 Commonwealth, 1980 Olympic, 1982 European and Commonwealth, and 1983 World Championship. His one defeat came in the 1978 European, and even then he came second with what was at the time a Commonwealth record.

His competitiveness is legendary, and never more so than in Helsinki in the summer of 1983, when, despite being far from fully fit after nagging injury, he trounced his arch-rival Jurgen Hingsen, the German who had usurped Daley's world record earlier in the season. No athlete is unbeatable, but that performance in the World Championships, when Daley piled up 8666 points in unfavourable weather conditions and was rock solid in each of the ten disciplines, must make his opponents despair. What must they do to beat him? The only man in history — in any event — to win World, Olympic, and European gold medals, has now gone four seasons without defeat in the decathlon.

And yet, for all his glowing achievements, one feels that Daley has still only scratched the surface of his ability. He may not get much better in the first two events of the decathlon, the 100 metres and the long jump, and he may never need to trundle round the 1500 metres faster than the 4:20.3 he clocked as a precocious and less heavily muscled 17-year-old. But there is much more to come in the other events, particularly in the throws.

For several years, Daley has made it known that he feels capable of scoring 9000 points one day, and no one can seriously disagree with that estimation even though it would represent a quantum jump in decathlon performance, the equivalent, perhaps, of a 3:45 mile. The breaking of records, though, is not what motivates Daley; for him, the sport — and it is his career, too, for he usually trains seven or eight hours each day — is all about *winning*. If it takes a record score to win, then so much the better.

It is this singleminded will to win that has been the hallmark of his career. A natural all-rounder, he took part in his first decathlon at 16, winning it with a remarkable total of 6685 points. He celebrated his 18th birthday competing in the Montreal Olympics, and was just 20 when he won his first gold medal, in the Commonwealth Games.

During his career, he has often fallen out with the media and with the administrators of the sport. He has been known to resent media preoccupation with middle-distance running and has scant respect for journalists who display a lack of knowledge about his event. He does not court controversy, but has been involved in his share of it. However, such are the charisma, the integrity, and the sheer talent of the man, that the public have always been willing to forgive the occasional gaffe. And although he has never competed in a decathlon in the land of his birth, one can understand his mistrust of English weather and his reluctance to waste the enormous amount of preparation he puts in for every decathlon he enters.

From his debut in 1975 up to the Olympic year of 1984, Daley Thompson has competed in 23 decathlons, and won 15 of them. In the chapters that follow, we have included on-the-spot reports of several of Daley's decathlons, all from *Athletics Weekly*. They are enthralling stories in themselves, even when Daley has led from start to finish, as the protagonists vie with each other to pile up the points. The decathlon is full of drama — the joy of producing a personal best when it matters most, the despair of failing to register a fair jump or throw, the supreme effort of dragging one's reluctant limbs round the track in the killer 1500 metres after two days of gruelling competition.

First, though, for the uninitiated, we have included an explanation of the decathlon and how it works.

The Decathlon

The decathlon consists of 10 separate track and field events, and is held over two days. Competitors earn points for their performances in each event, and the winner is the man with most points after the completion of the last event.

Decathlon calls for an extraordinary range of abilities. The events on the first day, in order, are: 100 metres, long jump, shot put, high jump, and 400 metres. The second day's events are: 110 metres hurdles, discus throw, pole vault, javelin throw, and 1500 metres. The decathlete must be careful that extra proficiency in his weak events — in Daley's case, the throws — is not achieved at the expense of other events. The balance of time and effort spent in training between different and often conflicting groups of events, and the attainment and maintenance of a physique compatible with all the unreasonable demands made on it, is the special and most intriguing challenge of the decathlon. In other words, not only do you not have to weigh too much for the running and jumping events, or too little for the throws, but you must adopt the right strategy in training. None of this is simple, and it requires complete dedication to the sport as well as enormous natural talent.

Daley Thompson has said that he does not find the actual competition physically demanding (although he could not deny that the last event, the 1500 metres, is usually a shattering physical experience). What is demanding is the mental effort needed to gear yourself up ten times in two days, each time trying to find the resources and concentration to run, jump, or throw just a little better than you have ever done before.

The word 'decathlon' comes from the Greek, meaning 'ten contests'. The ancient Greek Olympics included a pentathlon (five events), but the first decathlon was held in the United States in 1884, and it boasted such events as a half-mile walk and a hammer throw, all 10 events being held on the same day. This form of decathlon was included in the 1904 Olympics. The present decathlon became an Olympic event in 1912, and the current scoring tables were first drawn up in 1962. With minor revisions, these have been in use since then, although another major revision is due after the 1984 Olympics. A selection from the current tables may be found on page 96.

The programme of the decathlon means that competitors often have to get up about 5.00 am. This is because they need to eat their breakfast at least two hours before warming up, which they begin at about 7.30. The first event might begin as early as 8.30, and no competitor is allowed to leave the arena until the last event has been completed — perhaps 12 hours later. Officials accompany the decathletes everywhere, even to the toilet, to make sure that no forbidden substances are taken. Decathletes are lucky if they get to sleep before 11.00 pm, and then they are up at five again next day for a repeat performance.

2
SOMETHING SPECIAL

Daley (left), only 16 but with the physique of a man, en route to the English Schools 200m title in 1975.

It is often said, in retrospect, of people who have accomplished great things that they were born to be great. Daley Thompson has been described as a 'born competitor'. The first chapter in an autobiography (*One is My Lucky Number*) is, naturally enough, headed 'Born Winner'. Hindsight tends to exaggerate such claims. But from all reports, it is evident that there was something special about the young Daley. He was physically precocious, and his competitiveness and desire to win showed itself from an early age.

Daley was born Francis Morgan Thompson on July 30, 1958, in the Notting Hill district of London. His mother, Lydia, was Scottish. After World War II, in which she spent 4½ years in the Army packing equipment for soldiers, she settled down in London. Small, fair-skinned and blonde, she met and married Frank Thompson, a tall, handsome Nigerian who had spent most of his life in England. Daley grew up like his Ibo father. He had an elder brother, Franklin, and to avoid confusion — with three 'Franks' — their father gave young Francis a Nigerian name,

Ayodele. This became shortened to Dele, pronounced 'Daley' — the name in all the record books!

The young Daley was hyperactive and aggressively competitive, whether it was racing to finish a meal first or picking fights with bigger boys in his nursery school. From a baby, Daley was always on the go, never seeming to sleep. He was talking at twelve months, walking at fourteen. This boundless energy of his finally became too much for his mother when she also had a baby girl, Tracy, to deal with, and Daley was packed off to boarding school — at the tender age of seven. But even then, he was remarkably self-reliant. In a situation where other boys would be crying their eyes out, Daley treated it as an adventure. And, as always, he fell on his feet.

The school was Farney Close, at Bolney, about 13 miles north of Brighton. And sports were high on its curriculum. Daley was able to play football, his first love, five afternoons a week, and at weekends he was soon playing for local clubs. Daley threw himself wholeheartedly into everything he did. He excelled at everything, too, including his schoolwork. He was a good footballer, and had trials with Fulham and Chelsea. He became a great favourite of his headmaster, who was a sports fanatic. And this is a recurring pattern in Daley's life. Despite the fact that he was, self-confessedly, a 'bit of a trouble maker', cocky, and big-headed, his great charm and honest enthusiasm have always countered any bad impression he might have made, and people have gone out of their way to help him. His headmaster was no exception, providing the best facilities for Daley's football training and, in his last term at school, setting him on the path to his athletics career.

It was to keep Daley occupied, when he had little to do in his last term, that his headmaster took him down to Haywards Heath Harriers, the local athletics club. Daley was a natural sprinter, and from the start won all his races. After only a few weeks, he was competing in the English Schools Championships, in the 200 metres — and suffering the first of two or three blows to his ego. Hitherto unbeaten and confident to the point of cockiness, he finished only fourth. A few weeks later, on a miserable rainy day at Crystal Palace, he came sixth in the AAA Junior 100m and failed to make the final of the 200m. He admitted later that, sitting there in the stands, he had serious thoughts of giving up athletics and going back to football.

But, once again, there was a guardian angel to guide him — this time in the form of Bob Mortimer, a coach at Essex Beagles Athletic Club. Mortimer had watched him perform, and recognized his raw talent. He felt that, with proper coaching, Daley had the potential to be a good sprinter. Mortimer talked Daley out of quitting, and Daley joined Essex Beagles. In the couple of weeks that remained of the season, Daley made such an improvement that his confidence was restored. He has never looked back.

Daley left Farney Close at 15, with two 'O' Levels, and continued his studies at Hammersmith College of Further Education, gaining another six 'O' Levels. During the year, he trained regularly with Sussex Schools running coach Pete Thompson as well as at Essex Beagles, where Bob Mortimer continued to be the great influence on his career.

It was Mortimer who channelled Daley into decathlon. Believing that it was unwise for youngsters to specialize, and from the very first regarding Daley as decathlon material, he had him doing some high jumping and long jumping, and running in the 4×400m relay. But it was no easy task prising Daley away from his sprinting. He won the English Schools 200m and then the AAA Junior 100m, atoning for his failures the previous year. And he felt confident that he could get to the top in sprinting. He was really enjoying his athletics, competing for the Essex Beagles, and had no doubts now that this was going to be his career.

Bob Mortimer plugged away, coaxing, cajoling, and building up Daley's confidence in his all-round abilities. The decathlon was virtually a non-event in the UK, most of whose athletics heroes had been middle-distance runners, with the occasional sprinter and long-jumper thrown in. Peter Gabbett's UK record of 7903 points, set in 1971, was over 500 points adrift of the world's best. And the best British juniors were well over 1000 points behind the leading European juniors. Daley was very soon to change that in dramatic fashion.

Daley's problems were his weak events. His shot and

discus were poor, his hurdling awful, and he had an aversion to pole vaulting. It was in this last event that he showed his great courage, ignoring injuries and failure, eventually to make it one of his strongest events and jump higher than Britain's specialist vaulters. Gradually, almost imperceptibly, Mortimer won Daley over. In March 1975, he took him to train under Bruce Longden, who was the UK southern decathlon coach.

Longden, a man in his mid-thirties, had been coaching multi-events for ten years. He was immediately impressed with Daley. The basics of decathlon were there — good sprinting and jumping. Longden knew that good throwing could be taught. If the power was there, and it certainly was in Daley's case, then technique could be learnt.

Daley, who was still only 16, showed from the first that tremendous dedication that was to take him to the top. The sport was still a recreation for him, yet he trained hard every day. And that involved a great deal of travelling, whether it was right across London to Mayesbrook Park with the Beagles, where he worked on his running, or down to Crystal Palace for decathlon training with Bruce Longden. Daley chalked up several sprint wins at the start of the 1975 season, but results in *Athletics Weekly* also began to reveal that he was competing in the odd throwing event and the pole vault, and doing reasonably well, too. It was time, Bruce Longden thought, that Daley entered his first decathlon.

It was a low-key affair, the Welsh Open Decathlon at Cwmbran at the end of June. Longden took a group along from Essex Beagles. And as it was a meeting open to 18-year-olds and over, he had to get special dispensation for Daley, who was still a month off his 17th birthday, to compete. Daley covered the 100m in 11 seconds dead for a more than handy 804 points to start, and then long-jumped 6.99m, half a metre more than his previous best, for another 818 points. After this, all eyes were on this precocious youngster. There was a buzz every time he performed. There were not many spectators left for the last event, the 1500m, but all the athletes were there cheering Daley on. He finished up over 200 points ahead of the field. And although he had competed as a guest, athletes and officials agreed that he should receive the gold medal.

3
BREAKTHROUGH

Despite the excitement Daley's decathlon debut had created in others, he himself was still not sold on the idea. He still regarded himself as a sprinter. He enjoyed sprinting and the friendships he had made at the club, especially with fellow sprinter Dave Baptiste. Because of the pressures on Daley to concentrate on decathlon, the pair of them even considered joining another athletics club. The conversion, of course, came. But it was gradual, and Daley himself cannot say exactly when it happened.

He competed in his next decathlon at the end of August, again at Cwmbran. It was the AAA Junior Decathlon. Daley, who a month earlier had won the AAA Junior 100m title, amassed a remarkable 7008 points to win the Junior decathlon by over 1000 points! His score was enough to have won the senior title, staged at the same meeting and won by Pan Zeniou, a Greek Cypriot based in North London who was soon to become a great friend and training companion of Daley's.

The *Athletics Weekly* report put Daley's performance into fascinating statistical perspective:

> From the first event Daley Thompson looked as though he would end up with a great score, after clocking 10.7w in the 100m, a personal best time. He followed this up with a 7.21m jump (he recently jumped 7.30m). Nick Mason headed the shot performances at 12.17m with Thompson third overall at 10.80m. The high jumping was really first class, with six over 1.90m despite the windy conditions. Heading the parade was Ian Grant with a 1.98 clearance. Adrian Ord and Daley Thompson came next at 1.93m. Thompson exceeded his lifetime best in the 400m with a superb time of

49.6, to finish the first day of his second ever decathlon at 3880 — 116 pts ahead of his first day best when scoring 6685 in the Welsh Open Decathlon. John Davis was lying second at 3318.

Taking full advantage of the winds on the second day, Daley scored another personal best in the hurdles of 15.8, and then set his fourth personal best when throwing 32.20m in the discus. Chris Boreham, competing in his first decathlon, easily won the pole vault at 4.00m, and everything was set for the last two events. Daley's first throw in the javelin landed at 53.28m for yet another personal best, while Ord moved above Davis for second place. Daley achieved his 7000 target after he had won his sixth event (!), the 1500m in 4:36.5 (he needed 4:24.6 to equal Roy Mitchell's UK Junior record of 7088). He has another three years in the Junior age group (he was born on July 30th, 1958)! Daley's final points total of 7008, besides taking him into 2nd place on the UK Junior all-time list, gave him UK age records for 17- and 18-year-old, and he became the 14th Briton to exceed 7000.

Yet still Daley was not convinced. More arguments and heated discussions followed. Bob Mortimer felt that Daley's potential as a sprinter was limited, while his decathlon potential was as yet untapped.

Daley took part in his third decathlon at the beginning of October. He was selected to represent Great Britain in a Senior team event against France — the venue, Cwmbran, of course. And although he was beaten into second place by a Frenchman, Jean-Pierre Crozet, he showed impressive competitive qualities in compiling 7100 points. It was enough to break the UK Junior record by 12 points (he still had another two years in the Junior ranks) and to help the six-man team to a narrow victory over France (27,784 to 27,702 points). What is more, Daley chalked up no less than five personal bests — in the 400m, 110m hurdles, pole vault, javelin, and 1500m.

Daley was delighted with his performance but,

With coach Bob Mortimer, an early and continuing influence on Daley's career.

interviewed later that year, his major target for 1976 was to 'compete in a senior international other than a decathlon'. Yet, without realizing it, he had become a decathlete. It was not a conscious change. It just happened. And he has been a decathlete ever since.

The transformation from sprinter to decathlete called for a drastic change in training and life style. The results he had attained so far were largely the product of raw talent, tremendous effort, and his sheer competitiveness. Now all this had to be refined and channelled into the one complex event that the decathlon really is at the highest levels. Daley would need more than just the one training session a week with Bruce Longden. So he moved in with his coach. This meant transferring his studies to Crawley, too. He enrolled at Crawley College to study 'A' Levels. And he 'studied' decathlon virtually 24 hours a day. He was in his element, training, talking athletics, watching films on athletics. It was fortunate that Bruce's wife Sue was also an athlete.

Daley's target for 1976 soon became achieving the decathlon qualifying standard for the Olympics in Montreal. The 7650 points required called for an improvement of 550 points. Bruce and Daley gradually

Long-jumping for his club.

built up a rounded training programme that would produce just that kind of improvement. Daley worked tremendously hard. He threw himself into everything with his usual tenacity, but it was no longer a hobby — it was rapidly becoming an obsession.

During the winter of 1975-76, Daley trained six days a week. The programme included weights two or three times a week, and technical work aimed at developing his all-round ability, with emphasis on shot, discus, and pole vault. Other aspects of his training were fitted around the various venues — Crystal Palace, with its first-class running and vaulting facilities, the local Crawley Sports Centre for throws and weight training, and of course Mayesbrook Park, in Barking, home of the Essex Beagles.

Daley took part in several indoor meetings, running, jumping, vaulting. He achieved his first 4-metre pole vault in February. And at Cosford on 20 March, at the AAA Junior Indoor Championships, he won the 200m and long jump titles, came 2nd in the 60m and 3rd in the shot.

In his first decathlon of the season, Daley duly achieved the Olympic standard. It was the AAA Championship, and Daley chose to enter the Senior event. Yet again it was at Cwmbran, rapidly becoming Daley's 'home ground' (although this was to be his last decathlon in the UK). And it was another triumph for Daley, as Alan Lindop reported in *Athletics Weekly*.

> Those who were at Cwmbran Stadium over the weekend of May 22nd/23rd witnessed the best British decathlon ever, culminating in the finest all round performance by a 17-year-old and an Olympic qualifying standard. The event was the AAA Championship, also titled "The British Olympics Trials".
>
> Daley Thompson, who is not 18 until July 30th, opted out of the Junior competition, and was out to achieve the Olympic standard of 7650. He started off well with a personal best equalling time of 10.8, ahead of Gus McKenzie. Daley also headed the long jump with a personal best of 7.40/24ft 3½in. In the high jump, Daley equalled his best ever height of 1.98/6ft 6in on his third attempt, leaving McKenzie to go on and clear 2.04m.
>
> The first day finished with the 400, and Thompson strode out ahead to clock 49.1, against his best of 49.03. He had recorded 4092 to become only the third UK athlete to beat 4000, behind Peter Gabbett and Roy Mitchell.
>
> The second day started with a good hurdles win by McKenzie at 15.0, Thompson clocking a personal best of 15.5 to lead with 4889 from McKenzie (4699) and Mike Corden (4648). Six athletes threw the discus over 40m, while Thompson managed 38.78/127ft 3in. Thompson led with 5550 followed by McKenzie at 5219.
>
> With just the 1500 to go, a quick look at the tables showed that Corden had to do 4:14.7 and Thompson 4:25.2 for the Montreal standard. Snowy Brooks and Pan Zeniou decided to hot the pace up to give both Corden and Thompson a chance of achieving their goal. Zenny stayed there until the tape, finishing with 4:19.2, with Daley Thompson sprinting down the home straight, helped on by Phil Lewis, both

finishing in 4:20.3.
Daley had finished with 7684, 34 points over the standard, also beating his own UK Junior record of 7100, as well as Peter Gabbett's AAA National and UK All-Comers record of 7639. In addition, he had added 161 pts to Craig Brigham's world age-17 best. Daley now ranks third on the World Junior all-time list — and he still has another 19 months to go as a Junior!

Daley's performance earned him his Olympic place. It was the big breakthrough. He was interviewed a few weeks later by Dave Cocksedge for *Athletics Weekly*. His own version of that decathlon is more colourful than the essentially statistical record of Alan Lindop's. It is well worth reproducing, as it provides a wonderful insight into what goes on inside a decathlete's mind during the intensive two days of competition, and it reveals just how much the decathlon takes out of the athlete:

"They changed everything around on the first day so that we were running with the wind — it's great when officials do things for the athletes in meetings. Anyway, this wind was gusting all the time. We got settled in the blocks and it was blowing to 5 metres per second. It was a false start and when we got away with the second gun the wind had died to nothing. So I had to take a 10.8 when I felt that with a nice gust behind me I could have had a 10.6.

"The long jump? I was going well, there, really well. The 7.40 jump came on my third, when I'd got my run-up grooved. I made 7.11 on my first, 7.24 on my second and kicked out to 7.40 with my last chance. I was pretty pleased with that. The shot was disappointing. I've been throwing 13 metres indoors in training, but technically I have to stay with the shot every day or my technique really slides off. I lobbed the first one 12.74, then made my best of 12.79 on my second. My last one slid out the side of my hand and went only 12.58.

"In the high jump, I came in at 1.70, then made 1.80, 1.83, 1.89, 1.91, 1.94 and 1.98 feeling really good. That gave my confidence a shot after losing some points with the ball, but I missed at 2.01. Bruce feels that my high jump and 400 are pretty much on a par at the moment and these are the events I'm likely to improve very suddenly on. I keep running around 49 and that's a bit frustrating. I feel I've got a 48 in me somewhere, but it hasn't come out yet. Maybe it will in Montreal with the Games atmosphere. Anyway, they gave me 20 minutes to recover after the high jump and I ran 49.1, striding along easily."

Daley's overnight score was an impressive 4092, making him only the third UK decathlete ever to beat 4000 on first day. "But I wanted that 7650 Olympic qualifying score. That's what we'd been working for all winter. It all depended on me holding together on the Sunday. That first day was great, because we snapped through every event and everything fell into place nicely without the long delays and waiting about you usually get in decathlons. But the second day is always my hard day.

"I ran 15.5 in the hurdles which was about what I expected. Mike Corden and I were seeded together and we clocked the same time, diving through together. There's room for a lot of improvement in my hurdles. The discus wasn't anything great, but I was holding my chances of making 7650 with a 38.78. A week earlier at Haringey, I'd thrown 40.22, so this time I was hoping for something around 40 metres, but it didn't happen. My first throw was about 34 metres — lousy. I had to pull myself together. The second went 38.78 and the last one 38.76, so at least I was consistent. Then came the pole vault." He gives a grimace of disgust at the memory of clearing only 3.80. "I was fully expecting to make 4.00 or 4.10 from the way I'd been going in training, and from being psyched by my chances of winning and making the qualifying score. Jumping only 3.80 really put the pressure on me. I just wasn't riding with the pole after rocking back. I was trying to shoot through and clear the bar and I was pulling my legs out too quickly, which was dropping my hips. I was near caving in, there. It just shows you how you can lose a good score by making a few silly mistakes in one event and letting it get to you. I should have had 4.00 metres that day, at least. So it was down to the javelin.

"My first throw was around 54 metres; not bad but I wanted more. If I could get a 60 metre throw out, I'd only need to run 4:30 in the 1500 and if I can help it, I'd prefer not to absolutely kill myself in the 1500. So I put everything into my second throw. But I lifted the point at a critical moment, and it just went clear up into the air, nose-dived and came down about 20 metres away! I nearly fell apart. My face went white. I was near crying. I thought, 'You've blown it, Daley!' There was nothing for it but to get away and psyche myself up for my last chance. There were some tents pegged out there for us in case it rained and I went into one to be by myself for 10 minutes before my next throw. Bruce was there, but there was nothing he could do at that point. It was up to me. Somehow I got myself determined again and went back out to get that score together. I knew if I gave the jav away and settled for 54 metres I'd have to turn into John Walker for the 1500 and there was no way I could do that. I gave it a careful lob out and stayed loose and it went out to 56.92. Whew! Breathe again . . .

"Then there was just the 1500. I felt I had a chance now. I needed 4:25 to make the qualifying and my best was 4:32, but I knew I could go quite a bit faster if it was called for. The other lads were great. They got around me and paced me through the first two laps. Zenny (Pan Zeniou) took me through in 2:10 at 800 and the other lads were encouraging me all along the trackside. Tom McNab took over the public address and he was like a teenage kid, screaming for me to stay relaxed and push harder at the same time. When I think back, it was really funny. There was *some* atmosphere for that last event. All the spectators were yelling and I started pumping hard going into the last lap, chasing Zenny.

"I'd never have done anything like as fast as 4:20.3 without the other boys helping me along. They were great. They all deserve medals. We were completely wiped out at the end, lying around the track like we'd just been through a world war. It took me 15 minutes before I could get up and walk again; but knowing I'd beaten that 7650 made it all worthwhile. The pain doesn't matter when you know you've come through. I was on a high. Then came the anti-climax after another week, when I didn't train at all because, well, I just didn't want to. Then I had another week when I physically couldn't do anything. It was then I fully realised just how shattered I was. My body had taken a real caning, mentally and physically."

4
THE YOUNG OLYMPIAN

After the initial reaction to his efforts at Cwmbran, Daley soon got back into top gear. Three weeks later, he set a new Junior long jump record of 7.49m at Haringey, behind Alan Lerwill's Olympic qualifying leap of 7.89m. Daley had one more decathlon before the Olympics, an international match in Copenhagen at the end of June. And he experienced the nightmare of all decathletes — he 'zeroed' the pole vault. In other words, he failed all three attempts at his opening height and scored no points for that discipline. In a way, Daley was lucky. Disappointed as he was, having recorded three personal bests before the pole vault debacle, it was not an important decathlon. He finished 10th with 6639 points, a contribution substantial enough for the UK to win the match.

Competing in the Olympic Games was a marvellous experience for Daley, and he made the most of it. He drank in the heady atmosphere of Montreal. But he didn't allow it to cloud the issues. He was there to compete, and he performed well. And he was there to learn. He did this well, too.

The 1976 Olympic decathlon was a triumph for the popular American favourite Bruce Jenner. There was also a fine performance from the 1972 champion, Nikolai Avilov. And *Athletics Weekly* gave a fair amount of space to the promising performance of the 1980 winner as well:

> Bruce Jenner has claimed, for the past couple of years, to be the world's greatest all-round athlete; in Montreal he proved it to everyone's satisfaction. He never put a foot wrong in two days of competition against a field that included eight men with scores of 8200 or higher to their credit. In event after event he

Competing in the 1976 Olympics.

Bruce Jenner, Olympic victor.

reached out to personal bests in this his final competition. His score at the end — 8618 — added all of 164 points to Nikolai Avilov's Munich score, itself hailed as a monumental achievement.

Jenner wasn't the only man to distinguish himself. Guido Kratschmer, overnight leader with 4333, improved his national record to 8411 (only Jenner, Avilov and Bill Toomey have ever topped that) to stave off Avilov for the silver medal. He set personal bests in the high jump, 400, discus, pole vault and 1500. Avilov never quite recovered from a literally bad start. He was left in the 100 and could clock only 11.23 to leave him with an instant deficit of 70 pts compared with Jenner and 141 with Kratschmer. It was a struggle from then onwards to get on terms, though the defending champion gave it all he had, including his best ever marks in the shot and high jump. . . .

With Mike Corden withdrawing because of achilles tendon injury, Britain's sole representative was Daley Thompson, who started the contest aged 17 and a novice at this level, and ended as an 18-year-old with far greater insight into what world class decathlon competition is all about. He performed wonderfully well and but for a disaster in the javelin he might have placed as high as twelfth. His first day was marvellous, containing three personal bests: 100 in 10.79, shot of 13.10 and 400 in a gutsy 48.15. His halfway score of 4055 held 11th place of the 28 starters. "I'm really enjoying it," he enthused. "The atmosphere is great and everyone's been chatting to me. Bruce Jenner has been fantastic, pointing things out and being very helpful to me." Daley dropped away to 18th on the second day, but it was still a first-rate performance and he could derive much satisfaction from his breakthrough in the vault, up from 4.00 to 4.20.

Olympic Decathlon, Montreal 29/30.7.76

1	Bruce Jenner (USA)	8618	World Record
2	Guido Kratschmer (W. Germany)	8411	
3	Nikolai Avilov (USSR)	8369	
4	Raimo Pihl (Sweden)	8218	
5	Ryszard Skowronek (Poland)	8113	
6	Siegfried Stark (E. Germany)	8048	
18	**Daley Thompson (GB)**	**7434**	

(30 competitors)

Summing up his experience a few months later, Daley told *Athletics Weekly*: "It was just too unbelievable to take it all in in the time we were out there. Three weeks was too short for me. I couldn't get enough of it; I was like a kid with a new toy. But it was a learning experience I'll never forget for the rest of my life. I was in total awe of almost all the others there in the decathlon. I look up to men who can score over 8000 points because I know just how good you have to be to do that, and the scores out there were fantastic. Men were doing mind-blowing things, like Jenner, Kratschmer, Pihl, and Avilov. It has to be the best decathlon of all time so far, because seven guys beat 8000 points with electrical timing . . .

"The thing that came home to me most, I think, was the fact that all these other guys had their techniques down in every event so well that they could have done them backwards and blindfolded. As I've only been at this game seriously for two years, I haven't got that consistency yet. Let's face it, I'm still a novice and this was the Big League. . . . I was really excited in Montreal. Even after 14 hours of competing with these guys, I was up and had so much adrenalin going that I tended to rush things. But it was shattering. When it was all over, I don't think I've ever felt so tired. Not even when I first got that qualifying score in Cwmbran. It was emotional, mental, and physical fatigue and I was totally wiped out."

Daley didn't stay wiped out for very long. Just five weeks after the Games, he 'continued his meteoric ascent towards decathlon greatness' by setting a world Junior record of 7905 at Talence, in France, finishing fourth behind the Russian Grebenyuk in an international meeting. He beat the previous record (set by Austria's Josef Zeilbauer) by 63 points.

Asked (much later) how he had been able to put such a performance together after he had presumably peaked in the Olympics, he explained: "I am psyched for any decathlon and I knew I had better than 7684 (his previous best) in me. I felt I had a chance for 8000, if I could keep everything under control, and it was the perfect occasion for setting a personal best. The conditions were good, Grebenyuk was there, and Drut was there with the French Press all over him. There was a good crowd, and the officials were on the athletes' side." What must have given Daley an even greater incentive was the fuss being made of Drut, Olympic high hurdles champion who was trying his first decathlon. "Everywhere you looked, cameras were whirring and clicking, and he was the man they approached to ask how much rest we wanted between events."

Daley registered five personal bests, including a UK Junior long jump record. A mediocre javelin throw probably cost him the chance of achieving 8000; that and his inability to understand the French lap times in the 1500m! But he must have been pleased to win that event and finish ahead of Drut, who dropped out with cramp.

Anyway, there would be chance enough to compile the 'magic 8000' next season. And contemplating this next milestone in his career would give him something to think about during winter training.

5
THE MAGIC 8000

A decathlete's equipment — there are different shoes for each event.

Daley was not only becoming one of the greatest world-beating prospects British athletics had seen in years, but his extrovert personality was making him the reporter's dream. Newspaper and TV reporters flocked to him for quotes. And, at 18, he provided them with reams of copy — knowledgeable, perceptive, witty, and, above all, full of vitality and enthusiasm for his sport. Already, he knew decathlon inside-out. He knew all about his rivals. He knew exactly what he had to do to improve and how he was going to do it. And he knew what he wanted to do. For 1977, 8000 points was an obvious target, but his main aim, as always, was to win — in this case, the European Junior Championships.

First, though, there were the indoor meetings, and the individual events Daley used to complement his winter training. At Cosford in January, in the AAA Senior Indoor Championships, he placed 3rd in the 200m and 2nd in the long jump. Returning to Cosford in March for the Junior Championships, he stole the show:

> It was Daley Thompson's meeting. The 18-year-old UK decathlon record holder was all over the arena, turning the championships into a testing ground for his fitness and skill, as he calmly lifted three titles. He sprinted 60m in 6.9 three times, in heat, semi-final and final, outleaning Mike McFarlane who got away badly in the final after looking superb in his semi. Then Daley was pumping the 16lb shot a personal best of 14.32m for second place. Minutes after that he was entering the pole vault with the bar at 4.00m and clearing easily — he finished that event winning it at 4.40 to equal his outdoor best, and missing narrowly at 4.61. Then it was over to the long jump where he salted away his third title from 24 other rivals. A fairly tight programme kept him from contesting the hurdles, 200m and high jump also!

This was a fine springboard for Daley's decathlon campaign. The first decathlon was an international meeting in Austria. Every May, the tiny, peaceful village of Gotzis (population 2,000) comes alive when many of the world's finest decathletes gather there to compete in front of an enthusiastic and extremely knowledgeable crowd. It was to be the scene of future triumphs for Daley, not least in 1977, when he finished third but with a string of records to his name:

> Setting three new personal bests (in the 100,

long jump and hurdles) and equalling two others (high jump and shot), 18-year-old Daley Thompson opened his 1977 decathlon account on May 21st/22nd by smashing all officially recognised UK records with a score of 7921 pts. The record situation had previously been muddled: Peter Gabbett was credited with 8040 in the USA in 1972, but that mark was never ratified; Thompson himself had scored 7905 in France last year but, as with Gabbett's unofficial best, hand timing was used — a considerable benefit to the decathlete vis-à-vis electrical timing. The highest British score with electrical timing thus remained 7754 by Gabbett at the 1971 European Championships.

Daley's new score of 7921, achieved while placing 3rd in the Austrian open championship at Gotzis behind Sepp Zeilbauer and Fred Dixon, also constitutes a world junior record.

He made a brilliant start to the competition, running 100m in 10.71 (previous best electrical time of 10.79), long jumping 7.72m (25ft 4in) to break his own UK junior record of 7.57, putting the shot a useful 13.38m (pb of 13.59m) and high jumping 2.00m to tie another of his best performances. He completed the first day with 400 in 48.35 (he has run 48.00).

On the second day he clocked 15.24 for the hurdles, which was a massive improvement on his previous electrical best of 15.98 (though he had run 15.3 hand-timed), threw the discus 37.28m (pb of 41.80), vaulted 4.20m (pb of 4.40), tossed the javelin 55.78m (pb of 57.04) and covered 1500 in 4:23.8 (pb of 4:20.3). A vault of 4.40 and a 39m discus throw would have sufficed to take Daley over the 8000 barrier.

Daley was really on song now, and a month later in the searing heat of Madrid — shade temperature 30°C (86°F) — he inevitably broke the 8000 barrier, finishing a staggering 839 points ahead of the next man.

The swift rise towards the upper reaches of world decathlon stardom continues unabated for Daley Thompson, who does not turn 19 until July 30th. His latest and greatest exploit occurred in Madrid last weekend when he not only crashed through the 8000-point barrier but came very close to reaching 8200! Leading Britain to victory over Spain, Denmark and Italy, Daley piled up the colossal score of 8190 for a huge improvement (even allowing for the advantage of hand timing on this occasion) on his previous UK senior and world junior record of 7921 in Austria on May 21st/22nd. The performance ranks him second in the world this year, just 3 pts behind Aleksandr Grebenyuk (USSR), and he now occupies 17th place on the world all-time list.

During the two days, he set personal bests in the 100 (equal), shot, high jump, 400, 110 hurdles and pole vault. In the context of the recent UK Championships at Cwmbran, his performances in Madrid would have won him the 400 title, gained 2nd places in the high jump and long jump, and 3rd in the pole vault!

A month later, in the qualifying round of the European Combined Events Cup, at Sittard, in the Netherlands, Daley celebrated his 19th birthday with another outstanding performance. He won by over 500 points with a total of 8124. Although numerically less than his Madrid score, it was worth more because it was automatically timed. Daley himself was unaware at the time of this nicety of decathlon statistics in which hand-timing always produced 'better' performances, and was a little disappointed.

However, he went into his next competition, the European Junior Championships, with a great deal of confidence — too much, in fact. With scores in the 8000s, no fellow juniors were likely to bother him. But that's where he made his first big mistake. And he very nearly came a cropper.

6
BACK TO EARTH

With technical coach Bruce Longden.

Daley learnt a lesson in Donetsk, USSR, scene of the 1977 European Junior Championships; although, in the light of events the following year, he perhaps did not learn it well enough. So few have been the traumas in Daley's success-strewn career that they have become almost as well known as his triumphs. But nobody's perfect, and it would be a boring tale if winning came too easily or predictably. The lesson of Donetsk is that nothing is certain in athletics, least of all in decathlon.

Daley arrived in Russia with the 30-strong British team as just about the hottest favourite in the Championships. He had some 500 points to spare over his nearest rivals. But from the start the omens were unpromising. He did not like the food. He found the atmosphere depressing, and it was a long way from home. One would not have expected this sort of thing to bother Daley once he got onto the track, but it did seem to affect his concentration. Perhaps he had allowed a tinge of overconfidence to creep in and did not approach the competition with his usual meticulous attention to detail. Whatever the reasons, he got off to a terrible start, literally, when his blocks slipped in the 100 metres. He could record only 11.02s, his worst ever start to a decathlon and at least 80 points fewer than he might have expected. He disappointed in the next event, too, the long jump. The top jumper going into the competition, he performed nearly half a metre below his best. So after just two events he had virtually thrown away some 150 points. Fortunately, he recovered some of his composure in the next three events — no personal bests, but enough points to give him the overnight lead.

The rain was pelting down for the second day of the competition, but Daley made an encouraging start with a personal best of 14.95s in the hurdles, the first time he had cracked 15 seconds legally. His discus-throwing, however, did not live up to his recent improvements, and that was another 70 points gone. But it was his vaulting that really upset Daley. Having soared to 4.80 and 4.70m in his previous two decathlons, he could manage only 3.80m in Donetsk. That was some 250 points down the drain! The competition was slipping away from him. Daley, who never cried as a kid, left the field in tears.

He went to his room nearby — a breach of the rules which, fortunately for him, was ignored — and was on the verge of quitting the competition. After a dangerously long time, he decided to come out and give the javelin a go. He was well below his best again, but it was enough to keep him in contention.

Without burning up the track, Daley did what he had to do in the 1500m, and he won the competition by a mere 83 points. His score of 7647 points was some 500 below his best. He was fortunate in that there was no one in the field who was capable of taking advantage of his poor form. Ronald Wiese of East Germany came second (7564). In third place, just 40 points further back, was a West German giant called Jurgen Hingsen. He was, much later, to emerge as Daley's greatest rival. But Daley would never again give Hingsen such a great opportunity of beating him.

7
THE GOLD TRAIL

Commonwealth champion.

When Daley began his preparations for the 1978 season, he had gold in his sights. There were three major decathlons — at Gotzis in May, the Commonwealth Games at Edmonton and the European Championships at Prague, both in August. Daley was hundreds of points in front of his nearest Commonwealth rivals and an odds-on favourite for the gold medal at Edmonton. And if he continued to improve as fast as he had done in previous seasons, he would be in with a very strong chance at Prague.

There was no reason why Daley should not continue to improve apace. Each season, he was increasing his training, honing the various skills. He built his life round his training, and as a result his home arrangements had chopped and changed a great deal over the last few years. He had left home at 16 after falling out with his mother over his desire to take up athletics rather than find a regular job (his father had died three years earlier). He lived, at weekends, with a long-time friend of his mother's, Doreen Rayment, who had known him all his life. 'Aunt' Doreen not only provided bed and board, but often drove him to meetings, helped him with his track wear, looked after his correspondence, and cheered him on at competitions. Then there were the Pikes, a couple who treated Daley like an adopted son. He had moved out of the Longdens after about a year to share a flat in Crawley with friends. Shortly afterwards, a girl he was seeing invited him home, and her parents, Adrienne and Jack Pike, offered him their spare room to stay in. So now he had a permanent base in Crawley during the week.

To train and compete with the intensity and singlemindedness that was so essential to him, Daley needed all the help he could get. There was talk in 1977 that he might take up an athletics scholarship in the United States, but he valued his independence to compete when and where he wanted too much for that. In the summer of 1977, he received a grant under the Colgate Palmolive Sports Scheme, and later the British Amateur Athletic Board awarded him a small maintenance grant, 'enough to keep him in milk'.

Daley took a decision before the 1978 season to give up his studies at Crawley Technical College so that he could give himself completely to the decathlon. He reckoned sporting fame offered him a better chance of earning a living than adding further qualifications to the eight 'O' and two 'A' levels he already had. So in 1978 he was setting out on the gold trail in more ways than one.

At Gotzis in May, Daley gave firm evidence of his continuing improvement when he broke more records, although he did not win:

> Last year Daley Thompson kicked off the season with a Commonwealth and UK decathlon record of 7921 points when placing third at Gotzis in Austria. Daley returned to Gotzis on May 27th/28th and showed the extent of his continuing progress by placing second with the massive score of 8238 — and he's still only 19! The total broke his previous electrically timed record of 8124 as well as his manually timed best of 8190, and raises him from 17th to 12th on a combined world all-time list. Olympic silver-medallist Guido Kratschmer (Ger) won with 8410, just one point less than his Montreal score.
>
> Thompson piled up 4385 points on the first day (his previous best with electrical timing was 4324 on the way to his 8124 at Sittard last July), and was 51 pts ahead of Kratschmer at that stage. Daley opened with 10.77 for 100m, then long jumped the remarkable distance of 7.95m (26ft 1in)! Only three specialist British long jumpers have ever topped that: Lynn Davies, Roy Mitchell and Alan Lerwill. He proceeded with a put of 13.89m (his best in a decathlon), high jumped 2.03m and ran 400 in 47.76. Daley made an excellent start to the second day with a personal best of 14.85 in the hurdles, threw the discus 41.40m, vaulted 4.60m, threw the javelin 56.90m and

International Decathlon, Gotzis 27/28.5.78

1	Guido Kratschmer (W. Germany)	8410
2	**Daley Thompson (GB)**	**8238**
3	Josef Zeilbauer (Austria)	8105

completed a grand weekend's work with 4:29.11 for 1500.

How Daley's Marks Compared

Event	Best ever	Decathlon best	Gotzis
100	10.70	10.70	10.77
LJ	7.72	7.72	7.95
SP	14.53	13.84	13.89
HJ	2.07	2.07	2.03
400	47.31	47.31	47.76
110H	14.95	14.95	14.85
DT	41.80	41.70	41.40
PV	4.90	4.80	4.70
JT	59.02	57.04	56.90
1500	4:20.3	4:20.3	4:29.1

Kratschmer, obviously, was going to be the one to beat in Prague later that year. But first, for Daley, there was the Commonwealth Games. Daley took Edmonton by storm. He not only won the gold, but he won the hearts of the great Canadian crowd with a series of outstanding performances that were full of charisma. He was the star of the Games:

Decathlon: 1st Day

Daley Thompson hadn't been planning to chase any records in a decathlon which he was going to use as a tune-up for the really important item on the season's agenda, the European Championship, three weeks later. But from the moment when Daley opened with a fiery 10.50 for 100m, comfortably a lifetime best, there was no way he could bottle up his phenomenal talent. That sprint, assisted by a wind of only just over the limit at 2.23m/sec, was a full two-tenths faster than he had ever recorded before in decathlon competition, but Daley shrugged it off: "It wasn't bad, but I can do better."

Even Daley, whose towering ambition is matched only by his ability, was happy with the next event, the long jump. It was almost like watching Bob Beamon in Mexico City: a combination of ideal circumstances — in this case a gust of wind measured at 6.29m/sec, the relaxing warmth, and the uplift provided by a very large and enthusiastic crowd — conspired to create an act of athletic perfection. Daley looked as though he had found the secret of defying gravity as he soared to a monster of a jump . . . 8.11 metres! Even that almost unbelievable leap of 7.95w during his UK record score of 8238 at Gotzis in May had been made to look relatively ordinary, and this latest exploit actually broke Lynn Davies' Commonwealth Games record.

So, after two events, Daley already had 1973 points in the bag (101 up on Gotzis); it was the sort of start decathletes dream about. The one unfortunate aspect was that the wind in the long jump was over the 4m/sec limit which decathlon rules allow for the recognition of records, and thus whatever score Daley wound up with it would not be eligible for ratification. Asked what he thought that wind was worth to him in the long jump, Daley retorted: "About two centimetres — the rest was me." He decided to pass up his two remaining attempts, which was understandable as he was unlikely to top 8.11 and he needed to conserve energy. One could argue that had Daley recorded another good jump, and the wind had happened to be under the 4m tolerance, he could still have been in contention for an official record, but such considerations do not worry Daley. Anyway, the automatic wind gauge failed to function during the second round, while nine of the 12 jumps in the third round were aided by winds in excess of 5m/sec. One gust was measured at 11.76m/sec.

In the shot, Daley reached 14.43m, his first time over 14m in a decathlon, but that gave him little satisfaction. "It was bad. I did 14.70 five weeks ago." However, it did increase the margin over his previous UK record score to 134 points and that rose to 169 after high

At Edmonton, Daley equalled his personal best in the high jump, but was still not satisfied.

jumping 2.07m. That tied his all-time best . . . surely that would be acceptable even by Daley's demanding standards? Not at all. ''My run-up went to pot,'' he complained. ''I've jumped 2.10 in training and was expecting 2.14 today.''

The crowd, which had long ago taken Daley to its bosom, cheered his every move, and Daley — hamming it up as usual — was in his element. For the first time in his brief but remarkable career (remember, he only turned 20 the previous week) Daley was the focus of attention at a major Games, the star of the show. He loved it, and the fans loved him. Finally, to complete the most momentous day's work in decathlon history, Daley won his fifth consecutive event — the 400. His was a tremendous run in the blustery conditions, poorly rewarded by a time of 47.85. ''I lost maybe eight-tenths of a second because of the wind against in the back straight'' was his verdict, and no one could quibble with that assessment. As it was, his time — half a second outside his best — would have netted him 7th place in the specialists' 400m final. And thus came the reckoning . . . a monumental score of 4550 points to become the first man in history to top 4500 (with electrical timing) for the first day of a decathlon.

In a sense it was a one-man show, for Daley was over 500 points clear of the next man (Peter Hadfield), but in fact a prolonged battle was being waged for the other medals. Hadfield, who has scored over 7800 this year, ended the day just 4 points ahead of Graeme Watson, whose score of 4005 was 32 ahead of his previous best set on the way to his 7381 in the AAA championship. Far from out of contention, though, was Alan Drayton whose 3846 bettered by 26 pts his half-way mark in the AAA championship, which he won with 7424. Pan Zeniou, making history as the first athlete to represent Cyprus in the Commonwealth Games, was in 7th place with 3610 but with a strong second day to come.

First-Day Scores
1 D. Thompson (Eng) 4550; 2 P. Hadfield (Aus) 4009; 3 G. Watson (Eng) 4005; 4 A. Drayton (Eng) 3846; 5 Z. Smiechowski (Can) 3683; 6 R. Sadler (NZ) 3654.

Decathlon: 2nd Day

It was just three years ago that Daley Thompson tried his first decathlon. The result was sensational: 6685 points at the age of 16. A year later he was at the Montreal Olympics, part of the supporting cast as Bruce Jenner piled up that incredible score of 8618 points. Daley finished 18th in a field of 28 with a score of 7434. Two years later, back in Canada, and Daley — just turned 20 — is ready to attempt to beat Jenner's score, although he knows that because of excessive wind assistance in the long jump he cannot claim any official records. At the halfway stage, Daley's score is 4550, a world best, and he is far ahead of Jenner's 4298 at the corresponding point. He needs to be, for the American reeled off a phenomenal second day tally of 4320.

Daley's first event proved disappointing. He hits several of the hurdles ("bruised ankles, that's what I'm after", he joked later) and clocks 14.92, 7/100ths outside his best set at Gotzis, in finishing 2nd to Alan Drayton, who excelled himself with a 14.86 timing. In the discus, he has two poor throws under 40m before salvaging the situation with a toss of 41.68, which is only 12cm below his best ever. This is, however, one of his weakest events and, as he admits, "needs a lot of work". The pole vault is one of Daley's strongest specialities and he amasses 1005 points (not far short of the 1041 he collected for the 8.11m long jump) for his third-time clearance at 4.80m, which equals the highest he has ever vaulted in decathlon competition. With two events to go his score stands at 7130! He needs 1489 points from the javelin and 1500m to surpass Jenner, whereas his last two events at Gotzis when he set the UK record of 8238 yielded only 1318 (56.90m plus 4:29.1). But Daley still believed it was possible, for it could be done by throwing 65 metres and clocking a shade under 4:19. The only problem is that his personal bests stand at 59.42 and 4:20.3. However, a warm-up throw of around 62m gives Daley hopes of an imminent breakthrough. It is not to be: slipping because his spikes are too short, his first throw is a disaster: 45.88m. His second is better at 54.62 and his third goes 56.60, but it is a great disappointment to him. "I was throwing really badly" was his comment. So Jenner's score is safe, but there is still Nikolai Avilov's European record of 8454 to shoot for — a realistic target as Daley needs a time of 4:27.6

Daley shattered the Commonwealth Games decathlon record with his javelin throw — and he still had one event to come!

to top it. Daley, incidentally, has already shattered the Games record of 7492 with his nine-event score of 7849! Running the 1500 at full throttle, Daley passes through 400 in 68.7, 800 in 2:22.8 and the bell in 3:19.8 to finish in 4:25.8 and a brilliant total of 8467 points for second place on the world all-time list. Not a bad score considering, in Daley's opinion, he had only four good events — the 100, long jump, 400 and pole vault — while the 1500 he deemed reasonable!

It was a nice touch later when the decathletes took a communal lap of honour, arms linked (with the ever competitive Mr Thompson dipping as they approached the photo finish!), and the non-medallists formed an arc behind the top three as the medals were presented.

How Daley's Marks Compared

Event	Best Ever	Gotzis	Edmonton
100	10.65	10.77	10.50
LJ	7.95	7.95	8.11
SP	14.70	13.89	14.43
HJ	2.07	2.03	2.07
400	47.31	47.76	47.85
110H	14.85	14.85	14.92
DT	41.80	41.40	41.68
PV	4.90	4.70	4.80
JT	59.42	56.90	56.60
1500	4:20.3	4:29.1	4:25.8
		(8238)	(8467)

Commonwealth Games Decathlon, Edmonton 7/8.8.78

1	**Daley Thompson (England)**	**8467**
2	Peter Hadfield (Australia)	7623
3	Alan Drayton (England)	7484
4	Graeme Watson (England)	7261
5	Pan Zeniou (Cyprus)	7201
6	Rob Town (Canada)	7138
7	Robert Sadler (NZ)	7117
8	Charles Kokoyo (Kenya)	6775

(13 competitors)

The Commonwealth report was written before news from Germany had filtered through. Kratschmer, in his national championships, had compiled 8494 points to break the European record and put him second (to Jenner) on the all-time world list. So, had Daley's score been legal, it would not have been a European record. The scene was set, though, for a battle royal between Thompson and Kratschmer at Prague three weeks hence.

8
'FAILURE'

Daley hits the hurdles, and his hopes of European gold are jolted.

Losing the 1978 European decathlon was the most traumatic experience of young Daley Thompson's life. Psyching himself up to beat Kratschmer, Daley thought he had it won when his German rival pulled up injured in the very first event. But he let it slip. And his 'failure' in Prague has haunted him ever since:

> Decathlon: 1st Day
>
> The conditions (rain and wind) were not remotely comparable to Edmonton, but Daley Thompson was in an equally determined mood on the first day as he went about piling up his 288 point lead over his nearest opponent. This was not European record breaker Guido Kratschmer, as had been expected. The West German appeared at the 100m start line sporting a heavily taped right groin area — bearing out rumours that he had re-aggravated an old injury. His challenge to Thompson lasted exactly four strides. After that he pulled up in agony and limped disconsolately off the track. Daley, driving hard to a 'legal' decathlon

Daley (left) makes a fine start in the 100m, while Kratschmer (right) is just about to pull up.

best of 10.69, immediately turned around on finishing, saw his time and then looked back for Kratschmer. On observing his rival's plight, he whooped in glee and threw both arms skywards — an action that earned him boos and whistles from the Germans in the crowd.

Thompson's long jumping was up to scratch — he started with 7.81m before kicking out to 7.93 (wind: +0.5m) in the second round, his best ever without wind assistance. That gave him a two-event total of 1888 pts. Another decathlon personal best was soon to follow, when he punched the shot out to 14.69m on his opening effort and followed that up with another at 14.58. But Aleksandr Grebenyuk, with a 15.90 effort, had crept up to 2nd place with 2450 pts (Thompson 2658) and looked menacing. By the time the high jump started in the afternoon, the drizzle had turned to pelting rain, and jumping was hazardous. The end result: Thompson 2.04m, Grebenyuk 2.01, whilst Johannes Lahti went over 2.07. Points now were — Thompson 3549; Lahti 3324; Grebenyuk 3315.

The 400 saw the rare sight of Thompson headed to the line by a fellow decathlete. Dietmar Schauerhammer did the damage here in 47.59, with Daley lunging across the line a step behind him in 47.77. In the dismal conditions, that was fine sprinting and Daley's first-day total added up to a highly respectable 4459 digits — his best 'legal' score. Rainer Pottel was just two points behind Grebenyuk in 3rd place with Schauerhammer 4th on 4150. In fact, just 45 points covered 2nd to 7th!

Sipping a drink after his long day, Daley reflected: — "If I have the same sort of second day that I got in Edmonton, I'm in for gold; that is as long as someone doesn't come along with something ridiculous or if I get injured. Edmonton was good fun. This is business. This is the one that counts."

First-Day Scores
1, D. Thompson (UK) 4459; 2, A. Grebenyuk (USSR) 4171; 3, R. Pottel (GDR) 4169; 4, D. Schauerhammer (GDR) 4150; 5, J. Lahti (Fin) 4145; 6, H. Schmidt (Ger) 4132.

Decathlon: 2nd Day
On the second day, two near-disasters in the hurdles and pole vault cost Daley Thompson the title, although he showed his class by recovering well to keep a silver medal safe. Winner Aleksandr Grebenyuk, who has now beaten Daley four times, showed the sort of ultra-consistency that wins these major meetings: his two days' scores were 4171 and 4169! Contrast that to Thompson's 4459 and 3830. Event by event analysis:

110 hurdles: Thompson was out well, level with the powerful Soviet athlete over the first barrier. Then he clobbered the second hurdle hard, turned sharply sideways and almost lost balance. Somehow he got back into the race and safely cleared the remaining eight barriers for a dismally disappointing 15.28 against Grebenyuk's 14.43. That cut his overnight lead to 195 pts.

Discus: Grebenyuk had the lead briefly with a good opener of 48.42m against Thompson's 36.24. Then Daley pulled out yet another personal best of 43.52 for 754 precious points and 7-event total of 6032. His lead was now down to 105 pts, and Grebenyuk, a 73m man, had the javelin still to come. The situation was that, if each equalled their 1978 best marks, Thompson would win by 62 points. It all depended on the pole vault.

Pole vault: Thompson's casual approach may well be the culprit here. He neglected to measure up his pole against the bar on crucial attempts (and the standards were being constantly moved by other competitors). After clearing 4.20m with ease (his best is 4.90), he took 4.30 off with a trailing arm and thigh, and then had the pole bring the bar down after going well clear on a second try. His third desperate effort was a fluffed jump as he took it off with his calves on the way up. Meanwhile Grebenyuk was busy eating away into the lead with a 4.50 clearance (932 against 859). Grebenyuk then had trouble at 4.60, which cost him the lead — now down to 32 pts. Siegfried Stark, with a fine vault of 4.90, had moved into 3rd over Josef Zeilbauer. The scores were: Thompson 6891; Grebenyuk 6859; Stark 6709; Zeilbauer 6707; Schmidt 6668; Kutsenko 6608.

Javelin: Daley's first throw went out of the sector. Meanwhile Grebenyuk armed one out to 67.74m and it looked all over. But then Thompson showed the fighting qualities of a great athlete. Getting plenty of pull back, he unloaded a toss that measured 59.80 — a personal best. Grebenyuk had the lead now with 7712 against 7650. Stark had 7577 and Zeilbauer 7473. Silver seemed safe for the Briton, but he needed to get 8½ to 9 seconds clear of his big red-vested rival in the 1500 if he

A strong finish in the 1500m, but it is not enough.

wanted to snatch the gold medal by a point — a tall order.

1500m: In driving rain the decathletes set off on their 10th discipline, Grebenyuk keeping Thompson firmly in his sights. Stark led in 71 and 2:23, whilst Thompson followed, ever mindful of the Soviet athlete tailing him. He was running on the shoulder of Kutsenko, and every time he tried to edge past and take the running up from Stark, the Russian increased cadence and held him off. Into the final straight, Daley at last got the lead, only to have Kutsenko buffet and bore him almost onto the verge until he edged ahead in the last 40m. Grebenyuk (running a personal best) was just 1.6 sec behind Daley's 4:22.8 timing, and had his gold medal safe by 51 points. Such a show of bad sportsmanship by Kutsenko seemed unnecessary, and a protest ("an emotive one" claimed BAAB general secretary David Shaw) was filed but rejected. However, Thompson, with 4 personal bests, had a European silver medal and another UK record (legal scoring) by 51 points. And he had learned much.

He said afterwards: "Every time I went to go past him (Kutsenko) he blocked me; but I can't complain. I lost it myself in the hurdles and pole vault." Of the protest, David Shaw said: "I realise it has no chance, but I felt that the point had to be made that we were aware of the fact that the Russians were using questionable gamesmanship. If no one will back me up, I will pay the protest fee of 100 crowns out of my own pocket."

Grebenyuk said: "Daley is going to be a great competitor, but I knew that this time he was still too young and inexperienced to beat me. Moscow may be different — we must wait and see."

To say that Daley took his defeat badly is an understatement. He knew he had lost after the javelin, and was prepared to quit there and then. But he met

Daley congratulates Grebenyuk, but he knows he should have been up there.

European Championships Decathlon,
Prague 30/31.8.78

1	Aleksandr Grebenyuk (USSR)	8340
2	**Daley Thompson (GB)**	**8289**
3	Siegfried Stark (E. Germany)	8208
4	Josef Zeilbauer (Austria)	7988
5	Yuri Kutsenko (USSR)	7978
6	Roger Kanerva (Finland)	7945

(24 competitors)

Daley's European Defeat

	Grebenyuk			Thompson		
		Pts	Total		Pts	Total
100m	11.02s	799	799	10.69s	882	882
long jump	6.94m	808	1607	7.93m	1006	1888
shot	15.93m	843	2450	14.69m	770	2658
high jump	2.01m	865	3315	2.04m	891	3549
400m	48.88s	856	4171	47.77s	910	4459
110m hurdles	14.43s	912	5083	15.28s	819	5278
discus	48.42m	844	5927	43.52m	754	6032
pole vault	4.50m	932	6859	4.20m	859	6891
javelin	67.74m	853	7712	59.80m	759	7650
1500m	4:24.4	628	8340	4:22.8	639	8289

British team-mate Brendan Foster in the warm-up area, and the middle-distance star talked him out of quitting. Daley was in tears, but Foster persuaded him that a silver medal was better than a bronze, and a bronze was better than nothing. Even so, Daley was inconsolable for weeks afterwards. He should have had that gold medal, but someone else had taken it from him. What made him feel so desperately bad was that it was his own fault. He didn't perform to his best ability. That's why he felt almost suicidal.

He determined never to allow himself to be in a position where he would feel like that again. He determined to train harder and harder. Barring accidents, he would never lose again. Later he would appreciate that it was probably the best thing that ever happened to him. It was the supreme lesson, one he would never forget. He had learnt it, and now it was in the past. He would not want to learn lessons like that again. It helped him to calm down and channel his energy more carefully both in the build-up to competition and in the two days of the decathlon itself.

9
WORLD RECORD

However badly Daley felt about his defeat in Prague, the season had seen his transformation from a youngster with tremendous potential to a world star. The Commonwealth gold had brought him fame and public acclaim. And at least most of his fellow countrymen had now heard of the decathlon, even if they were still hazy as to what it was all about. For once, the media concentration on middle-distance running worked to his benefit, because the talking point after Prague was not his defeat but that of Ovett and Coe by Olaf Beyer in the 800 metres. At the end of the season, Daley was voted male athlete of the year by the British Athletics Writers' Association, the first decathlete to be so honoured.

Daley enjoyed his new-found fame. He was recognized wherever he went. His easy manner and ready wit made him a natural public performer. He was deluged with requests for interviews, invitations to open this and that and to make TV appearances. Most important, though, was the fact that his financial worries were over. The grants, aid, and sponsorship that poured in would enable him to travel, train, eat, live, and compete in complete freedom. The BAAB provided more substantial support for training and equipment. Various sponsors provided free use of a car, unlimited air travel, and free meat. And although he turned down countless offers from American universities, he accepted an invitation to tour some of them early in 1979. He trained at San Diego University under the warm Californian sun, and has since spent two or three months there every winter in ideal training conditions.

Back home, Daley and Aunt Doreen moved into a small house in Worcester Park, south-west of London and much nearer Crawley. Apart from her work with children in Kensington, she continued to help organize Daley's public life away from athletics — the interviews and appearances. He did what he could, but he never let it interfere with his decathlon.

Daley had not planned to enter any decathlons in 1979. He competed every weekend for his club in individual events, often in several at the same meeting. His goal was the 1980 Olympics in Moscow. He even missed Gotzis. Bruce Longden, however, was uneasy about such a programme. Eventually Daley decided to compete in the West German decathlon at Flein at the end of July — and he came close to breaking the world record. His first-day score of 4507 included personal bests in the 100m (10.45s), the shot (14.82m), and the 400m (47.30s). After the first event of the second day, a 14.39s hurdles that knocked nearly half a second off his previous best, the chances of breaking Jenner's world record looked bright. But after a good effort with the discus, disaster struck in the pole vault. Daley, whose poles had been lost on the flight over, had to use a borrowed pole; not surprisingly in the circumstances, he failed his opening height of 4.30m. He gave vent to his feelings with a personal best in the javelin, but he did not bother to take part in the 1500m.

Daley continued his Olympic build-up with individual events, and at the end of August he won a half-decathlon at Crystal Palace that included his first 5-metre pole vault, ironically with an untried pole. This novelty event condensed the decathlon second-day events into a shorter period of time, so Daley's 3917, equalling his previous best (when winning at Edmonton), was a fine performance. Indoors at Cosford in November, he put the shot over 15 metres for the first time — not once, but three times.

Wintering in San Diego from February to April, Daley returned in tremendous form. He had one decathlon lined up before the Olympics. It was sensational:

> Thompson Breaks Jenner's World Record
>
> Still only 21, and competing in the 16th decathlon of his astonishing career, Daley Thompson fulfilled the first of his great athletic ambitions last weekend when at Gotzis in Austria he replaced Bruce Jenner as world record holder. He surpassed the American's Montreal Olympic score by just five points with a total of 8622 points. Had he run the 1500m

eight-tenths of a second slower, or had his 100m time been 10.58 instead of 10.55, or had he raised his high jump personal best to 2.10m and not 2.11, he would have failed in his quest — it was that close. But he succeeded, gloriously, to become a worthy inheritor of Jenner's mantle as the world's greatest all-round athlete. Like Jenner in Montreal, Thompson was pushed to new heights by Guido Kratschmer (who, alas, will not be in Moscow to challenge Thompson, Stark, Grebenyuk etc for the Olympic crown). Here is how the Gotzis competition unfolded for Daley . . .

100m: Fastest with 10.55 (919 pts), compared with his personal best of 10.45. Long jump: Surprisingly, he placed only 3rd with 7.72m (965 pts) — his legal best is 7.93 — but still a very sound start. Shot: Far from his 15.45m indoors, he reached only 14.46 (756 pts), but maintained his overall lead over Kratschmer, 2640 to 2602. High jump: The key to Daley's ultimate triumph, as it was with Mary Peters in Munich, he raised his best from 2.07m to 2.11 (950 pts). 400m: Fastest at 48.04 (896 pts), but below the expectations of a man who has run 47.30.

Overnight leader with 4486 pts (as against 4550 at Edmonton in 1978), and ahead of Germany's Jurgen Hingsen (4337) and Kratschmer (4305), Daley would have to score at least 4132 pts on the second day to break the record — and his best second-day score to date was only 3917.

110m hurdles: Just the start he needed: a personal best of 14.37 (previously 14.39), worth 919 pts, although Kratschmer was faster with 14.16. Discus: Lost ground here also to Kratschmer with a moderate throw of 42.98m (743 pts) — well below his best of 45.22. Running scores: Thompson 6148, Kratschmer 6050. Pole vault: Daley 'won' what is one of his strongest but most crisis-prone events with 4.90m (1028 pts), only 10cm below his best. Javelin: For a realistic shot at the record, he had to throw farther than ever before (62.34m) . . . and he obliged with a very timely personal best of 65.38 (826 pts). 1500m: Daley's best time, set back in 1976 when less heavily built than he is now, is 4:20.3. With his score at 8002 pts for nine events, he needed a time of not slower than 4:26.1 to break Jenner's record. He ran 4:25.5 (4:25.49) for a place in the history books. Oh yes, he also gained the Olympic qualifying standard he hadn't previously achieved!

International Decathlon, Gotzis 17/18.5.80

1	**Daley Thompson (GB)**	**8622**	**World Record**
2	Guido Kratschmer (W. Germany)	8421	
3	Jurgen Hingsen (W. Germany)	8276	
4	Josef Zeilbauer (Austria)	8196	
5	Yuri Kutsenko (USSR)	8195	
6	Aleksandr Nevskiy (USSR)	8056	

Thompson's world record compared with Jenner's in 1976 *(Adjusted to 1977 revision)*

	Jenner			**Thompson**		
		Pts	**Total**		**Pts**	**Total**
100m	10.94s	819	819	10.55s	919	919
long jump	7.22m	865	1684	7.72m	965	1884
shot	15.35m	809	2493	14.46m	756	2640
high jump	2.03m	882	3375	2.11m	950	3590
400m	47.51s	922	4297	48.04s	896	4486
110m hurdles	14.84s	866	5163	14.37s	919	5405
discus	50.04m	873	6036	42.98m	743	6148
pole vault	4.80m	1005	7041	4.90m	1028	7176
javelin	68.52m	862	7903	65.38m	826	8002
1500m	4:12.6	714	8617	4:25.5	620	8622

Less than a month later, Kratschmer took Daley's world record by 27 points at Bernhausen. It was a great pity that he would not be in Moscow for what would have been a classic duel.

10
OLYMPIC CHAMPION

Daley Thompson arrived in Moscow with five years of hard work behind him. No one could have been better prepared. Even the uncertainty over whether Britain would be sending a team could not unsettle Daley, who seemed to put the boycott issue right out of his mind. He had got over a temporary loss of edge suffered as a reaction to his somewhat premature world record performance two months earlier. He was now quietly confident. There was no one in the competition who could beat him — except himself. And the lesson of Prague had been well learnt.

The Olympic boycott had thrown a cloud over the Games. The Soviet invasion of Afghanistan in December had triggered off a reaction in the Western world, led by the United States, that resulted among other things in the withdrawal of more than twenty national teams, including the United States and West Germany. The British Olympic Association resisted pressure from the government, insisting that politics should not be allowed to interfere with sport. As that sentiment can hardly be equated with holding the Games in a totalitarian state in the first place, it might be said that the BOA refused to join the boycott for the wrong reasons. As far as the decathlon was concerned, the absence of the United States had no bearing on the result, but Kratschmer and Hingsen of West Germany would be missed. Daley, however, had beaten them comprehensively in Gotzis, and there was no reason to believe that either could have reversed that result.

Twenty-one competitors turned out on Friday, 25th July, to start the first event. Where gold was concerned, 20 of them might just as well have joined the boycott:

> Decathlon: 1st Day
> What a day it was for British athletics, for in addition to Wells' golden success Daley Thompson was well on his way to winning the decathlon — and with a possible world record. He enjoyed a superb first day for a halfway score of 4542 points. That was just 8 pts short of his record Edmonton total but 66 in advance of his world record figures of 8622 at Gotzis and 82 ahead of Guido Kratschmer's score in his later world record of 8649.

Cool, blustery conditions greeted the decathletes for the start of the 100m but that didn't affect Daley too much. He won his heat by a six-metre margin in 10.62 — only 2/100ths slower than Cameron Sharp achieved in the 100 semis later in the day. That was a good enough start but it paled by comparison with his long jump performance . . . a mighty second round leap, into a 1.37m/sec breeze of exactly 8 metres! That was worth 1020 lovely points and would have been good enough to place him 4th in the 1976 Olympic long jump proper. It was his best ever legal distance and he became only the third Briton (after Lynn Davies and Roy Mitchell) to jump 8m without wind assistance. Another fine result followed: a shot put of 15.18m, easily his best ever in decathlon competition. Thus, after three events his score was 2719 (12 in advance of Kratschmer's corresponding mark) and he was already 232 pts ahead of his nearest rival, Yuriy Kutsenko. With two of Thompson's most formidable opponents, the East Germans Siegfried Stark (ankle injury) and Rainer Pottel (three long jump fouls), having dropped out after two events, it was clear that only the Russians remained as possible challengers — and they were far behind at this stage.

Daley pulled further ahead of world record schedule with what he described as a "so so" high jump of 2.08m, a height he has bettered only once before in decathlon competition. He failed at 2.10, due he thinks to losing concentration after six or seven hours of competition. Hoping to run close to 47 sec for 400m, he had to settle for 48.01, hampered by the swirling wind which Daley claims was against him both in the back straight and home straight. His halfway lead was a yawning 264 pts over Kutsenko, with the other two Soviet contestants close behind.

On the Saturday, the long-awaited clash between Ovett

and Coe took place. It resulted in a 1-2 for Britain, with Ovett the victor. Coe, who had been favourite to win the 800m, was as disconsolate with his silver medal as Daley had been in Prague. For Daley, though, Moscow was a different story:

> Decathlon: 2nd Day
> Later in a memorable evening another British athlete struck gold when Daley Thompson fulfilled his destiny: to be Bruce Jenner's successor as Olympic decathlon champion. It was a shame that world record holder Guido Kratschmer was unable to compete, but Daley was in such cracking form that there is little to suggest that the German would have been any more successful against Thompson than was the case when they clashed at Gotzis earlier in the summer.
>
> Daley's overnight lead of 264 points was so substantial an advantage that it was practically impossible for anyone to beat him. Only Thompson himself could do that, but he enjoyed a solid, disaster-free day which gave no hope at all to his opponents. His final winning margin of 164 pts would have been appreciably larger had he wished to push himself to the limit in the 1500m. Instead he took it relatively easy, savouring the delight of an ambition achieved.
>
> Hopes of a world record fizzled out because of the weather. It was pouring in the morning, and, after slipping over on the warm-up track, Daley ran the hurdles somewhat cautiously. Instead of the 14.1 he had been hoping for, he had to settle for 14.47 — a tenth slower than in Gotzis but a good, sound performance. He was still ahead of Kratschmer's world record pace — 5449 to 5432 — but fell behind for the first time after the discus. The throwers were doubly handicapped, by a slippery circle as well as greasy implements, and in the circumstances his best of 42.24m was very reasonable. After 7 events, Thompson's score

was 6178 as against Kratschmer's corresponding 6223 and Daley's own 6148 at Gotzis. More to the point, though, was that his closest challenger, Valeriy Katschanov, with a 14.40 hurdles and 46.02m discus, had narrowed the gap to 198 points. Imagine the Russian's frustration as well as pain when he pulled a calf muscle on the runway attempting his opening height (3.60m) in the pole vault. Weeping with disappointment, he was forced to withdraw.

All went well for Daley, happily. Coming in lower than usual for safety's sake, he vaulted well and was easily over 4.70m before failing at 4.80. His score was now 7159 (Kratschmer 7180) and his lead over second-placer Yuri Kutsenko a resounding 326 pts. Kutsenko followed up his 4.90 vault with a good javelin throw of 68.08m to narrow the gap to 280 pts, Daley throwing a solid 64.16 for a 9-event score of 7970 — 49 short of Kratschmer at that stage. A world record was still a possibility, but it would need a formidable personal best of 4:17.2. But victory was certain as long as Daley broke 5 minutes. Understandably, instead of risking blowing up in pursuit of the world record he settled for a steady run at the back, taking 4:39.9, far behind Kutsenko's 4:22.6. Four days before his 22nd birthday, Daley Thompson was Olympic champion with a score of 8495 — the fifth highest total in history.

Olympic Decathlon, Moscow 25/26.7.80

1	**Daley Thompson (GB)**	**8495**
2	Yuri Kutsenko (USSR)	8331
3	Sergei Zhelanov (USSR)	8135
4	Georg Werthner (Austria)	8050
5	Josef Zeilbauer (Austria)	8007
6	Dariusz Ludwig (Poland)	7978
7	Atanass Andonov (Bulgaria)	7927
8	Steffen Grummt (E. Germany)	7892

(21 competitors)

Olympic first three after each event

100m	1 Thompson 900	2 McStravick (GB) 812	3 Hadfield (Aus) 795
lj	1 Thompson 1920	2 Kutsenko 1728	3 Kachanov (USSR) 1703
shot	1 Thompson 2719	2 Kutsenko 2487	3 Kachanov 2474
hj	1 Thompson 3644	2 Kutsenko 3412	3 Kachanov and Zhelanov 3399
400m	1 Thompson 4542	2 Kutsenko 4278	3 Kachanov 4265
110m h	1 Thompson 5449	2 Kachanov 5180	3 Kutsenko 5122
discus	1 Thompson 6178	2 Kachanov 5980	3 Zhelanov 5844
pv	1 Thompson 7159	2 Kutsenko 6833	3 Zhelanov 6801
jav	1 Thompson 7970	2 Kutsenko 7690	3 Zhelanov 7529
1500m	1 Thompson 8495	2 Kutsenko 8331	3 Zhelanov 8135

Victory ceremonies in Moscow were muted as no national anthems were played because of the boycott. But British fans greeted Daley's triumph with a rendering of 'God Save the Queen', and Daley conducted the singing from the rostrum.

Daley confirmed afterwards that, despite the prospect of attractive offers to cash in on his fame (as his predecessor Bruce Jenner had done), he would continue in athletics. "I love this game. I really do love every minute of it. I intend to compete in the next two Olympics. No decathlete has ever won three golds so I couldn't wish for a better incentive. I won't even be 30 at the 1988 Games. Why stop doing something that's fun?" Asked about commercial gain, Daley, irrepressible as ever, retorted: "I'm open to offers — might make a few blue movies!" Asked about not regaining the world record, Daley said: "I came here to win the gold medal. I've won it. The rain really spoilt any world record chances." It would be another two years before he did get a chance.

11
A NEW RIVAL

Daley won back his world record at Gotzis, with the towering Hingsen 175 points behind. Hingsen was to take Kratschmer's place as Daley's biggest rival.

After his Olympic victory, Daley allowed himself a small celebration with his Aunt Doreen and friends, and then went off to holiday on remote islands, out of the public glare. But he was soon back to work — the only work he knows, training for the decathlons to come. There would be the European in two years and the first World Athletics Championships in three. First, though, there was the world record that Kratschmer had taken from him. Records have never been Daley's first priority, but it would give him great satisfaction to win it back.

Daley planned an assault on the record in June 1981 at a multi-events international in Canada. It was the UK against Canada in senior and junior decathlons and senior and junior heptathlons (the women's seven-discipline event). The sun had blazed down on the prairie town of Saskatoon for days before the meeting, with virtually no rainfall for months. Then, on the first day of the meeting, it bucketed down. Despite the adverse conditions, Daley had compiled a marvellous 4505 points by the end of the day, hoping for a change in the weather for the second. But it was worse. The hurdles were delayed because of water in the timing system, but still Daley ran a respectable 14.81. When a driving wind blew the pole vault indoors, all hopes of an official record were gone. Daley produced his first 5-metre vault in a decathlon, threw a fine javelin, but only started the 1500m so that his score would be valid for the match. His 7936 points from nine events was more than enough to give the UK victory. It was also enough to win him the individual honours — by more than 300 points!

That was Daley's one and only decathlon in 1981. He controversially opted out of the European Multi-Events Cup Final — a showpiece decathlon held in Birmingham, one in which Kratschmer was competing. He received a great deal of criticism for missing this. But he liked to make his own arrangements. He was still a great club man, competing for Essex Beagles in scores of events every year. But Daley was going through a difficult period. He was beginning to tire of the trappings of stardom, resenting his loss of anonymity in public. And he was dissatisfied with his coaching arrangements. He had progressed away from Bruce Longden as the Olympics came and went, and felt he needed more than he was getting from Andrzej Krzesinski, the Polish coach, at Haringey. He was hungry — ravenous — for improvement, especially in his weaker events.

Daley wintered in the Californian sun as usual, and his exploits in 1982 more than made up for the barren 1981 season. He first hit the headlines again in May:

Daley Regains World Decathlon Record

Daley Thompson is world record holder for the decathlon again. Competing in the renowned annual international event at Gotzis in Austria on May 22nd/23rd, Daley added 58 points to Guido Kratschmer's figures as he amassed a score of 8707* points. His own previous best, which had stood as world record for just 27 days in 1980, was 8622 — also set at Gotzis. Last weekend's decathlon was the first he has completed since his Moscow Olympic triumph.

A back strain sustained in the second event, the long jump, and unfavourable weather conditions on the second day prevented Daley from smashing the record by a much bigger margin. As he remarked at the end: "It justifies the work I've put in over the last four months, but I'm not as good as I could be. I can improve all round and the 9000 points barrier is possible." His next decathlon would be at the European Championships in Athens in September, where he expects his closest opponent to be Germany's Jurgen Hingsen, the runner-up at Gotzis with 8529 points. Colin Boreham, who will represent N. Ireland in Brisbane, finished 8th with the magnificent score of 7935 (to rank 2nd on the UK all-time list using fully automatic timing), and Pan Zeniou, who will wear the colours of Cyprus, was 15th with a near-best of 7547.

Daley set another 'world record': a massive first day score of 4632** points, made up of 10.49*** for 100m (his legal best is 10.45), a

* Later adjusted to 8704 points.

** Later adjusted to 4629 points.

*** Later changed to 10.50 seconds.

7.95m long jump (8.00 is his best wind-free leap), a put of 15.31m (1 cm below his outdoor pb), a 2.08m high jump (he has cleared 2.11 outdoors and 2.14 indoors) and a superb lifetime best of 46.86 for 400m (previous fastest of 47.30), in which he covered the first 200 in 21.6!

A second personal best came in the first event of the second day: 14.31 for the hurdles, a 6/100ths improvement. He then threw the discus 44.34m (he has done 47.44), vaulted 4.90m in the rain (as against 5.20), hurled the javelin 60.52m (65.38) with a foul of close to 64m, and — needing around 4:39 for the record — clocked 4:30.55 for 1500m, a distance he once covered in 4:20.3 when his bodyweight was somewhat lower.

International Decathlon, Gotzis 22/23.5.82

1	**Daley Thompson (GB)**	**8704**	**World Record**
2	Jurgen Hingsen (W. Germany)	8529	
3	Grigori Degtaryev (USSR)	8247	
4	Stephan Niklaus (Switz)	8176	
5	Siegfried Wentz (W. Germany)	8136	
6	Walter Kulvet (USSR)	8060	
7	Dave Steen (Canada)	7980	
8	Colin Boreham (GB)	7935	

(33 competitors)

Daley was right to think that Hingsen would be his closest opponent in Athens. Although Kratschmer was not competing, his tall compatriot was showing signs of overtaking him. And Daley was soon to find out in dramatic fashion that he had a new rival.

12
SETBACKS

The pole vault has no fears for Daley even after his accident.

Looking back to 1982, the season when Daley established himself without any shadow of a doubt as the world's supreme all-round athlete, it is hard to believe that he suffered a serious injury that kept him out of action for most of July.

Since his world record triumph at Gotzis, he had continued his programme of competing in club events for the Essex Beagles, and it was in a league match at Copthall, in London, that disaster struck on July 3rd. He had already won the 100m and hurdles and was attempting 5.20m in the pole vault. After one good effort, his second attempt felt good, but as he soared up, his pole snapped. It had happened before, more than once, and is an occupational hazard of pole-vaulters, with their bendy fibreglass poles. This time, however, the broken, jagged shaft badly gashed his left arm, his right thumb was broken, and his knee, in his own words, was 'done in as well'. His left arm was stitched and put in plaster to stop him bending his elbow. It was a sorry state to be in with the European Championships looming up in just two months. Then, just as he was getting back into shape again with some solid club performances, the news came through that Hingsen had beaten his world record.

At the German championships in mid-August, Hingsen had amassed a total of 8723 points, just 19 more than Daley's Gotzis mark. So now, not only had Daley to struggle to get back to peak fitness for Athens, but when he got there he would have to surmount the challenge of his biggest rival at the top of his form. The scene was set for an intriguing contest, one that all followers of athletics were looking forward to with great relish.

13
THOMPSON SUPREME

Victor and vanquished.

Daley was quietly confident when he reached Athens. He not only wanted the European title, but he wanted his world record back. Hingsen was confident, too; or at least he tried to give the impression of confidence. He might have taken Daley's record, but he had never beaten Daley. He was all too well aware of this.

Before the Championships got under way, the IAAF congress at Athens made two important decisions. They established a category of meeting in which athletes could get paid appearance money. And they introduced the concept of athlete's funds, by which means any money earned by athletes through appearances, sponsorship, or promotional activities would go into a fund administered by a body affiliated to the IAAF, in Britain's case the British Amateur Athletic Board. The athlete would be able to draw what he needed from his fund to enable him to train and compete. This covered virtually everything, from equipment, travel, food, and accommodation to medical treatment and coaching. And it meant that stars such as Coe, Ovett, Cram, and Daley Thompson could not only devote all their time to athletics without any hardship, but could build up a substantial nest-egg for their retirement.

Not that Daley had any thoughts of retirement. As usual, mind and body were concentrated on just one thing — winning the decathlon. This is how Mel Watman described it in *Athletics Weekly*:

> Decathlon: 1st Day
> Daley drew first blood with his 10.51 100m, which was a fair start, but Hingsen's left a lot to be desired, as he ran outside 11 seconds. Both men performed below par in the long jump, Hingsen, though, perhaps more than Daley, as he reached only 7.58m compared to the Essex Beagles' 7.80 winner. Daley was already away to a great 171-point lead after only two events!
>
> Hingsen, a 16m man, had the chance to pull back a few points in the shot, but, as with his earlier events, the result was disappointing — 15.52, while Thompson, to the clear delight of the crowd, produced a superb decathlon best of 15.44 to keep the German's gain down to only

four points. Thompson's put was only 1cm short of his absolute best, and as Frank Zarnowski, 'Track and Field News' decathlon expert, declared, "at 12.44 on the first day, it's all over," and most present were inclined to agree with him!

From seemingly plain-sailing, though, the event became a competition, as Daley went crashing out of the high jump, clearing only 2.03m, while Hingsen went up and up, to 2.15. On paper, he still had a better second day than Thompson to come, and, as though in defiance of the high jump, Daley lashed out round the 400m in a great 47.11, after passing 200m in 22.5, to increase his 66 point lead to 114 overnight.

Further down the field, Stephan Niklaus was the best of the rest and was third overnight with 4295 from Sigi Wentz on 4227, but neither of them had any hope of making an impression on the two 'big boys'.

Daley was not too exhausted after his first day's work to give the media a few comments: "I was well pleased with the first day's work and although any chance of a world record is out of the question, I'm confident that I can keep it up and win the gold." Happily, Daley was right about winning the title . . . and equally happily he was quite wrong about the world record being out of his reach. His first-day score of 4549 might have been 83 points down on when he set his former record of 8707 at Gotzis, but what he didn't bargain for was that he would tot up a prodigious second-day score of 4194:

Decathlon: 2nd Day

Daley opened the second day with a vengeance, and clocked a grand 14.39 in the high hurdles, not far short of his all-time best, although Hingsen showed that he was still just as determined with a 14.61 win, faster than that set in his world record. The next event, the discus, was one in which Hingsen should have taken more points from Thompson. And up to the end of the second round, this was the case, as Daley had registered only 39.82m to the German's 42.68. With the final throw, though, the true competitiveness of the man came through, and he unleashed a 45.48 to which Hingsen could only respond with 44.72.

Barring a disaster, Daley wasn't going to lose any points in the vault, and, although Hingsen cleared a good 4.80m, it wasn't enough to match Daley's 5.00, which won him his pool and was the equal highest with Sigi Stark. By now, Daley's lead was a fairly comfortable 199 points, with Stark back in third on 6950 to the two leaders' 7307 and 7108.

Another throwing event, the javelin, also went to Thompson, and his 63.56m was too far in excess of Hingsen's 60.42 to give the German any hope now. The winner of the pool was Georg Werthner with a good 70.60, while Stark consolidated his bronze medal position with 67.38 in third. It was quite amazing;

Hingsen (255) turns at the finish of the 1500m to find Daley right behind him, an easy victor overall. Kratschmer (on the left) helped push Daley to a new world record.

Daley does a lap of honour with the flag after his magnificent performance.

Daley had all but won the competition and needed a 4:26.4 1500m to recapture the world record, in a competition where he hadn't set a single pb!

Boreham took the first heat with a great last lap effort, and Thompson followed suit with a gutsy 63.5 last 400, befitting the spirit of the man who proved that he is undoubtedly the best in the world at the hardest all-round discipline in the sport. He clocked 4:23.71 to wrest the record back, and became the first man in any event to hold Olympic, European and Commonwealth titles, as well as the world record.

What a performance — and it all took place in the torrid 90° heat of Athens' Olympic Stadium. The 1500m was magnificent, as even rival Guido Kratschmer urged Daley on during his fantastic last lap. And Daley stood there at the end, towering over his beaten and exhausted opponents who were lying flopped out on the track. The scoreboard flashed the magic words 'World Record', and Daley celebrated with a lap of honour, waving a huge Union Jack.

European Championships Decathlon, Athens 7/8.9.82

1	**Daley Thompson (GB)**	**8743**	**World Record**
2	Jurgen Hingsen (W. Germany)	8517	
3	Siegried Stark (E. Germany)	8433	
4	Steffen Grummt (E. Germany)	8217	
5	Georg Werthner (Austria)	8171	
6	Grigori Degtaryev (USSR)	8160	
7	Valeri Kachanov (USSR)	8116	
8	Christian Gugler (Switz)	8035	
9	Guido Kratschmer (W. Germany)	8016	
10	Atanass Andonov (Bulgaria)	7904	

(27 competitors)

The European Championship Duel

	Thompson (led from 1st event)			**Hingsen** (2nd from 2nd event)		
100m	10.51s	930	930	11.01s	802	802
long jump	7.80m	980	1910	7.58m	937	1739
shot	15.44m	815	2725	15.52m	819	2558
high jump	2.03m	882	3607	2.15m	983	3541
400m	47.11s	942	4549	48.10s	894	4435
110m hurdles	14.39s	916	5465	14.61s	891	5326
discus	45.48m	790	6255	44.74m	777	6103
pole vault	5.00m	1052	7307	4.80m	1005	7108
javelin	63.56m	804	8111	60.42m	766	7874
1500m	4:23.71	632	8743	4:22.22	643	8517

14
CONTROVERSY AND HONOURS

Francis Morgan Thompson, MBE.

Daley's golden boy image was tarnished soon after his European triumph when he declined to carry the flag at the opening ceremony of the Commonwealth Games in Brisbane. It was an incident that was blown up out of all proportion, but it was not the first time that he had fallen foul of authority. And as before it was due largely to lack of communication, a certain arrogance on his part, and the eagerness of certain sections of the Press to make a meal of any little story they can get their hands on.

The earlier contretemps had centred on his failure to compete in the European Cup at Birmingham in 1981. The previous year, the BAAB had asked Daley to guarantee his appearance in this event, or his Sports Aid Foundation grant (then £4,000 a year) would be stopped. Daley replied that he never guaranteed anything. His aim in 1981 was to recapture his world record. As a result, he lost his grant, and the BAAB refused him permission to compete at Gotzis that year. When, having promoted the Birmingham meeting as if he would be competing, they asked him to do so (a month before the event), he declined. His absence was an embarrassment for the Board, and a disappointment for the public. It could have been handled better, and Daley certainly did not deserve some of the Press he got.

The flag incident also caused bad feeling. He was accused of being unpatriotic. There were implications that he 'rejected the honour' out of resentment, because he was the only one of the Moscow gold medallists not to figure in the honours lists. Daley repudiated these criticisms. He defended his decision to decline the honour, explaining that his meticulous build-up to an event did not include standing in the sweltering heat for four hours. He would not do anything to jeopardize his chances. England team manager Andy Norman felt that Daley had his priorities wrong. He described Daley's singlemindedness as 'tunnel vision'. "The only thing he can see," he said, "is the decathlon."

As things turned out, Daley could probably have carried the flag while competing in the decathlon, and still won it! He overwhelmed the opposition by over 400 points, which would have been considerably more had he not been content to jog round the 1500m at the back of the field. Any record aspirations he might have had were

Long-jumping in the heat of Brisbane.

thwarted right from the start by the windy conditions. He had to contend with a headwind in the 100m and again in the hurdles the following day. The wind also lost him points in the 400m and the pole vault, in which he did not try to improve on a successful 4.90m jump. He finished with 8410 points, routine for him, but a total achieved only by a handful of others in the world. Daley came first in five events, second in four, and trotted in ninth in the 1500m.

Commonwealth Games Decathlon, Brisbane 4/5.10.82

1	**Daley Thompson (England)**	**8410**
2	Dave Steen (Canada)	8004
3	Fidelis Obikwu (England)	7726
4	Peter Hadfield (Australia)	7511
5	Peter Dyer (NZ)	7316
6	Charles Kokoyo (Kenya)	7118
7	Greg Haydenluck (Canada)	6766
8	Colin Boreham (N. Ireland)	6727
9	Pan Zeniou (Cyprus)	6273
10	Cornelius Kemboi (Kenya)	6176

(15 competitors)

Daley led the field on a lap of honour, as he had done four years earlier at Edmonton. But, still peeved at his treatment over the flag incident, he declined to talk to the Press afterwards. Nevertheless, he was later voted Athlete of the Year again by the British Athletics Writers' Association. That is something they could hardly deny the Olympic, European, and Commonwealth champion, who had gone one better than sixties long-jumper Lynn Davies because he also held the world record.

That wasn't the end of the honours for Daley. He was also named Sportsman of the Year by the British Sportswriters' Association, and he won the coveted BBC Sports Personality of the Year award. And to cap it all, he was awarded the MBE in the Queen's New Year's Honours List.

Looking back, 1982 had been quite a year for Daley, despite the controversies. But Daley wouldn't be looking back. He would be looking forward to 1983, and the first World Athletics Championships.

15
WORLD CHAMPION

The final score at Helsinki, no world record but another marvellous display by Daley. (The scoreboard has not caught up with Hingsen's world record set two months earlier!)

The introduction of the World Athletics Championships has added a new dimension to the sport. On a par with the Olympics, it doubles the meetings every four years when the world's greatest athletes come together in competition. The first World Championships were scheduled for Helsinki in 1983, the second for Rome in 1987.

Daley's build-up to Helsinki suffered in exactly the same way as his preparation the previous year for Athens — first injury and then the loss of his world record to Hingsen.

The injury hit Daley in February, during an indoor pentathlon in Toronto. He felt a severe pain in his lower back after landing in the long jump pit and had to withdraw from the competition. He was jarred so badly (the sand was too shallow) that he spent the next four days on crutches. The injury wrecked his spring training programme to the extent that he could not run for nearly two months. Daley played the injury down, and said he would be competing in Helsinki come what may, because he did not need to be 100 per cent fit to win. But he had to scrap plans for competing in Gotzis.

Meanwhile, he returned to Britain to begin competing in club events in May. At the same time, he went to Paris to collect yet another honour, the Grand Prix de l'Academie des Sports, awarded for the single outstanding exploit in the year. Seb Coe had been the only other Englishman so honoured. He also signed a lucrative contract with Fabergé, to join the likes of Kevin Keegan and Henry Cooper in promoting Brut. His other commercial contracts included Lucozade health drinks and Hertz hire cars. In addition, there were television programmes to take part in, all contributing to the Daley Thompson fund. He needed an agent now to look after his interests, not an easy task when Daley's only interests are the ten events making up the decathlon, and any other considerations must take a back seat however great the sum involved.

Hingsen wrested the world record away from Daley, for the second time, in the West German World Championships Trials at Bernhausen on June 4/5. His score of 8779 exceeded Daley's mark by 36 points. He was pushed all the way by Siegfried Wentz, whose 8718 total was the fourth best ever. With Kratschmer coming third, West Germany would be sending a formidable trio of decathletes to Helsinki.

Daley was presented with a swift opportunity to regain his record when he competed in Toronto two days later, but his attempt was foiled by windy conditions and lack of competition. His performance was encouraging, however, the total of 8509 being deceptive in that he loitered round the 1500m in 4:42.6. His pole vault, 5.10m, was his best in a decathlon.

The World Championships took place in August and were a huge success, both in organization and performance. The stars included sprinter/long-jumper Carl Lewis, and middle-distance runner Mary Decker of the United States, Czechoslovakia's powerhouse of the track Jarmila Kratochvilova, Britain's Steve Cram and, of course, Daley Thompson:

> Decathlon: Daley's Demolition Job
>
> A favourite pastime of track & field fans the world over is comparing the merits of various athletes. That's difficult and provocative enough when simply discussing contemporaries in the same event; when extended to weighing up the achievements of athletes from any event and era it's just impossible . . . which doesn't stop us trying!
>
> Who is the greatest British athlete of all time, as measured by his or her record of international successes? Names like Douglas Lowe, Sydney Wooderson, Mary Rand, Lynn Davies, David Hemery, Steve Ovett and Seb Coe leap to mind, but after his astonishing demolition job on the highly touted German opposition in Helsinki there is now no doubt in my mind — writes Mel Watman — that Daley Thompson tops them all. His sheer competitiveness and coolness under pressure is without parallel.
>
> The man cannot countenance defeat (it's five years since he last lost a decathlon, and that was a traumatic experience for him), yet he put himself on the line in Helsinki in facing up to a

gruelling contest with a superbly trained and in-form world record holder in Jurgen Hingsen, while he himself could not possibly have been at his very best after struggling to recover in time from injury. Actually, it was touch and go right up to the last moment whether Daley would take part but, after being snubbed by Hingsen and Siggy Wentz in the athletes' village, he couldn't wait to take them on!

First Day

Having made the decision to compete, Daley knew he had to strike a psychological blow by piling up the points in his strong early events. That he did, and the opposition never quite recovered. Put yourself in Hingsen's shoes: he's the world record holder, he's been showing the best form of his life in recent competitions, and all he's heard about Daley in recent weeks has been negative . . . striving to regain fitness after a groin strain which in turn followed a back injury, uncertain even whether he's going to compete in Helsinki. Hingsen naturally feels confident, the glint of that gold medal already in his mind's eye.

In reality, though, the German giant has built a false sense of security. For Daley does show up, and in the first event, the 100, shows no sign of any physical problems as he races to a 10.60 clocking, a gaping 3½ metres clear of Hingsen. Straight away he's 89 points ahead. That's a blow to Hingsen, but he can console himself with the thought that the long jump is next and that he's cleared 8.00 this year while Daley can point to only 7.63. Conditions are unfavourable for good jumping — it's cool and it's raining — and Hingsen is pleased with his opening leap of 7.75, all the more so when Daley fouls. But his sense of well-being vanishes in the second round when he fouls and Daley comes through with a monster jump of 7.88, the best by any British athlete this season. Instead of closing the gap, Hingsen finds himself further behind . . . 114 pts.

Don't panic, thinks Hingsen. The shot is next and he's put over 16m, whereas Daley has yet to reach 15½m. But although he does gain, putting 15.66 to his rival's 15.35, he's unhappy. His final effort of around 15.80 is ruled a foul, much to his disgust, and so he picks up only a paltry 18 pts. He trails by 96. Thank goodness, he feels, that it's time for the high jump. As a 2.18 performer, he can count on pulling back a good number of points. At least he thought he could, but an attack of cramp holds him down to a mere 2.00, while Daley — though also well below his best — clears 2.03 and widens his advantage to 121 pts. Hingsen is shattered, if not as distraught as medal contender Grigoriy Degtyarov (8538 this year) who fails to clear any height at all. The only bright spot of Hingsen's first day — and likewise Daley's only faltering moment — comes in the final event, the rain-soaked 400. The Olympic and European champion can usually be relied upon to win in fast time, but on this occasion his less than desired state of fitness lets him down and he fades in the closing stages to place fourth (48.12) in a blanket finish. Hingsen wins in 48.08, a fine run for him, but all the effort gains him precisely one point vis-à-vis Thompson. The first day scores: Thompson 4486, Hingsen 4366, Torsten Voss 4314, Uwe Freimuth 4237, Wentz 4234.

Second Day

If Hingsen starts the second day thoroughly demoralised, Thompson — although elated by his solid lead — is equally worried as he confronts the hurdles. Because of his injuries, he hasn't been able to carry out any preparation for this event, and he's aware that all that previous good work could be swept aside. Daley's fears prove groundless, for not

Despite his lack of practice, Daley stays within a whisker of Hingsen in the hurdles.

only does he get close to his fastest ever time with 14.37, but he finishes only inches behind his arch-rival (14.36) and thus forfeits just one digit in a discipline which he reckoned would be considerably more costly. That potential crisis safely behind him, Daley picks up more bonus points in the discus. He improves on each trial to 44.46, less than earth shattering but very useful indeed compared to Hingsen's best of 43.30 — a disastrous return for a man who has thrown over 48m. Daley's lead is now 141 pts, and Hingsen's only hope now is that his opponent will bomb out in the vault. No chance! Daley is in full flow and succeeds in clearing 5.10 (equalling his best ever in a decathlon) with daylight to spare. Hingsen matches his pb of 4.90, but can't prevent Daley's lead stretching to 188 pts.

The awesome competitive drive of Thompson can be seen also in the javelin. After two rounds, he trails by a huge margin, 60.44 to Hingsen's lifetime best of 67.42, but with his final attempt he comes through with the second longest throw of his decathlon career —

65.24. His broad smile says it all. When you're hot, you're hot. Thus, as the curtain rises on the final act of the drama — the 1500m — Daley's score is 8075, Hingsen's 7913. As Daley would need to run 4:14.1, over 6 sec inside his best, Hingsen's world record of 8777 is safe — but so too is the gold medal for Daley. Hingsen would have to finish some 22 sec ahead of Daley, and although he runs bravely to clock 4:21.59, it is nowhere near what is required, as Daley lumbers around his last lap in 69 sec for a 4:29.72 timing.

With a total score of 8666, Daley wins by 105 pts, with Wentz — a strong second-day exponent (he 'won' the hurdles in 14.13 and the javelin with a spectacular 75.08) — taking third. It wasn't Daley's top-scoring decathlon, but it was probably his greatest.

Only 80 per cent sure of competing until the last moment, Daley said afterwards that he would have stopped if one event had gone badly: "I wasn't fully fit and my concentration was bad because of my groin injury. The pain became especially bad during the last two events."

Hingsen sportingly accepts defeat; Daley allows himself a smile of triumph.

Hingsen took his defeat sportingly and deserves the last word: "I came to win, but in the end I'm satisfied with my silver medal because Daley is truly the greatest among us, for he has no weaknesses."

World Championships Decathlon, Helsinki 12/13.8.83

1	**Daley Thompson (GB)**	**8666**
2	Jurgen Hingsen (W. Germany)	8561
3	Siegfried Wentz (W. Germany)	8478
4	Uwe Freimuth (E. Germany)	8433
5	Stephan Niklaus (Switz)	8212
6	Aleksandr Nevsky (USSR)	8201
7	Torsten Voss (E. Germany)	8167
8	Steffen Grummt (E. Germany)	8149
9	Guido Kratschmer (W. Germany)	8096
10	Dariusz Ludwig (Poland)	7982
11	Trond Skramstad (Norway)	7827
12	Robert De Wit (Neth)	7769
13	Martin Machura (Czech)	7639
14	Conny Silfver (Sweden)	7527
15	Thrainn Hafsteinsson (Iceland)	7356
16	Josko Vlasic (Yug)	7329
17	Angel Diaz (Guatemala)	6239
18	Niulolo Pelesikoti (Tonga)	5332

(25 competitors; 7 did not finish)

World Championship 'Shoot-out'

	Thompson (led from 1st event)			**Hingsen** (2nd from 3rd event)		
100m	10.60s	906	906	10.95s	817	817
long jump	7.88m	996	1902	7.75m	971	1788
shot	15.35m	809	2711	15.66m	827	2615
high jump	2.03m	882	3593	2.00m	857	3472
400m	48.12s	893	4486	48.08s	894	4366
110m hurdles	14.37s	919	5405	14.36s	920	5286
discus	44.46m	771	6176	43.30m	749	6035
pole vault	5.10m	1075	7251	4.90m	1028	7063
javelin	65.24m	824	8075	67.42m	850	7913
1500m	4:29.72	591	8666	4:21.59	648	8561

16

THE PRIVATE DALEY THOMPSON

On the surface, Daley Thompson's character seems to be a contradiction in terms. He has an extrovert personality, yet thinks deeply about himself. He is at ease in front of the TV cameras, making commercials or programmes, yet shuns the limelight. But Daley has always been a private person. And as his fame has grown, he has found an even greater need to preserve his privacy. He has no taste for the goldfish bowl existence of the superstar. As a result, at home he rarely goes out anywhere. The simple act of eating a hamburger in a fast-food restaurant becomes an ordeal. Kids follow him around the shops. People shove paper and pencil under his nose for his autograph. Daley dislikes all this. He has never regarded himself as public property.

He also resents the intrusion of the media into his private life. And he tends to give the sporting Press short shrift if they display an ignorance of the decathlon, as some often do. Rightly or wrongly, he has a chip on his shoulder about the attention paid to middle-distance runners in Britain. He doesn't envy their fame — he doesn't need to — but he feels that decathlon does not get its fair share of reportage.

Daley has never allowed his success to go to his head. He has always valued his friendship with fellow athletes such as discus thrower Richard Slaney, sprinter Dave Baptiste, and decathlete Pan Zeniou, regardless of their success or lack of it. And he is quick to acknowledge their part in his own achievements. When competing in major championships, he enjoys the company of team-mates, chatting away and encouraging them. He will help and advise a newcomer to competition, just as Bruce Jenner found time to talk to him at the 1976 Olympics.

His concentration when competing is legendary. Just as he found the decathletes in 1976 performing their various skills automatically, he is now able to pack all his concentration into the few seconds before he makes his effort. This is the result of years of training and perhaps months of 'psyching himself up' for an event. He is a master, also, of the most potent form of gamesmanship, the art of keeping his opponents guessing. Like a poker player, he holds his cards close to his chest. He keeps quiet both about injuries and training performances, letting his rivals do the worrying.

Daley rarely takes time off from decathlon, and when he does it's usually in the form of an outdoor sport such as scuba diving.

All this makes him the most formidable of opponents. As Hingsen said, he has no weaknesses. His simple philosophy is not to give his rivals a ray of hope. The Thompson-Hingsen rivalry looked in danger of becoming a feud at the World Championships, such hostility being rare among decathletes. But a chance meeting on the Canary Islands over the New Year seems to have put it back on a friendly basis.

Daley has never regarded the time he puts into training as a sacrifice. Decathlon is his life. The people closest to him know this and respect it — both friends and girlfriends. As he has often said, a night out with him is a trip to the cinema and a hamburger and fries. He regards hard work in training as money in the bank, something to draw on when, as happened in his last major competitions, he has been carrying an injury. He used to say that competition was his life — as a kid, he had to be first in everything, from finishing a meal to catching a bus. Now he channels all this into the decathlon.

As the years have gone by, so Daley's confidence in himself has grown. It has always been high, but the quality and depth of his training has made it more so. It is a confidence that must not be confused with complacency. For Daley is never satisfied, never one to dwell on past performances. No matter how well he performs, he will always find something he can improve on.

To give himself more training time, Daley went to California early in 1984 to prepare for the Olympics. Interviewed by Jon Hendershott of *Track and Field News*, he explained why he had gone over three months earlier than usual: "The reason I'm in California now, living and training, is that the weather is so bad at home and I want to be in such good shape. My commitment is such that I know I'm okay at the moment, but I would like to be better. The extra couple of hours I can put in every day might be reflected in my scores at the end of the year."

Already, at meetings in California, he has registered personal bests in the shot and the 100 metres — a sobering thought for his rivals in Los Angeles in August. And he is still learning little lessons. On February 12th in Toronto, he lost an indoor pentathlon (60yd hurdles, long jump, shot, high jump, 1000m) by 11 points to Dave Steen of Canada, who also broke Daley's world's best for this event with a score of 4108 points. Daley was terribly upset about it, not because he lost but because he felt that for the first time in his life he had not *tried* his best — he high-jumped only 1.90m. He had performed below his best before, but not for want of trying. The lesson he learnt from that competition was that "I took too much for granted and I have to concentrate. I can't just go in and expect things to happen. I'm just like everybody else." A week later, Daley recaptured his world mark with a score of 4219 at Canyon, Texas.

It can be no consolation at all to his Olympic challengers that Daley is still learning — and learning so fast.

17
APPENDIX

Daley Thompson's Decathlons

1975

1) **6685 points 1st** Welsh AAA & Open Decathlon, Cwmbran 28/29 Jun

11.0	6.99	10.74	1.97	50.2	16.8	31.42	2.90	51.88	4:31.0
804	818	514	891	797	676	506	498	658	583
804	1622	2136	2967	3764	4440	4946	5444	6102	6685

2) **7008 points 1st** AAA Junior Championships, Cwmbran 30/31 Aug

10.7w	7.21	10.80	1.93	49.6	15.8	32.20	3.30	53.28	4:36.5
879	863	518	796	824	767	523	615	676	547
879	1742	2260	3056	3880	4647	5170	5785	6461	7008

3) **7100 points 2nd** GB-v-France (Seniors), Cwmbran 4/5 Oct

10.8w	7.11	11.77	1.90	49.3	16.0	31.84	3.40	57.04	4:30.9
853	842	584	769	838	748	515	644	724	583
853	1695	2279	3048	3886	4634	5149	5793	6517	7100

1976

4) **7684 points 1st** AAA Senior Championships, Cwmbran 22/23 May

10.8	7.40	12.79	1.98	49.1	15.5	38.78	3.80	56.92	4:20.3
853	901	651	840	847	797	661	754	723	657
853	1754	2405	3245	4092	4889	5550	6304	7027	7684

5) **6639 points 10th** GB-v-Netherlands-v-Spain-v-Denmark, Copenhagen 26/27 Jun

10.6	7.26	11.94	1.93	48.6	15.3	36.46	NHC	51.34	4:41.2
905	873	595	796	871	817	614	000	651	517
905	1778	2373	3169	4040	4857	5471	5471	6122	6639

6) **7434 points 18th** Olympic Games, Montreal 29/30 Jul

10.79	7.19	13.10	1.91	48.15	15.98	36.36	4.20	45.18	4:29.55
857	859	671	779	889	750	612	859	566	592
857	1716	2387	3166	4055	4805	5417	6276	6842	7434

(7436 points on 1977 tables — 48.15 (891pts) (4057 points — 1st day).

7) **7905 points 4th** International Meeting, Talence, France 4/5 Sep

10.5	7.57	13.59	1.95	48.1	15.4	37.70	4.40	51.92	4:24.9
932	935	702	813	893	807	639	909	658	617
932	1867	2569	3382	4275	5082	5721	6630	7288	7905

1977

8) **7921 points 3rd** International meeting, Gotzis 21/22 May

10.71w	7.72	13.38	2.00	48.35	15.24	37.28	4.20	55.78	4:23.8
877	965	689	857	880	823	631	859	708	632
877	1842	2531	3388	4268	5091	5722	6581	7289	7921

(7922 points on 1977 tables — 48.35 (881pts) (4269pts — 1st day).

9) **8190 points 1st** GB-v-Spain-v-Denmark-v-Italy, Madrid 25/26 Jun

10.5	7.60	13.85	2.07	47.4	15.1	39.60	4.80	50.32	4:29.0
932	941	719	917	928	837	678	1005	637	596
932	1873	2592	3509	4437	5274	5952	6957	7594	8190

10) **8124 points 1st** European Cup Semi-Finals, Sittard, Holland 30/31 Jul

10.70	7.54	13.84	2.01	47.31	15.26	41.70	4.70	54.48	4:30.4
880	929	718	865	932	821	719	981	692	587
880	1809	2527	3392	4324	5145	5864	6845	7537	8124

11) **7647 points 1st** European Junior Championships, Donetsk, SU 19/20 Aug

11.02	7.25	13.72	2.06	47.59	14.95	38.22	3.80	49.72	4:35.53
799	871	710	909	918	854	650	754	629	553
799	1670	2380	3289	4207	5061	5711	6465	7094	7647

1978

12) **8238 points 2nd** International Meeting, Gotzis 27/28 May

10.77	7.95w	13.89	2.03	47.76	14.85	41.40	4.60	56.90	4:29.11
862	1010	721	882	910	865	713	957	723	595
862	1872	2593	3475	4385	5250	5963	6920	7643	8238

13) **8467w points 1st** Commonwealth Games, Edmonton 7/8 Aug

10.50w	8.11w	14.43	2.07	47.85	14.92	41.68	4.80	56.60	4:25.78
932	1041	754	917	906	857	718	1005	719	618
932	1973	2727	3644	4550	5407	6125	7130	7849	8647

14) **8289 points 2nd** European Championships, Prague 30/31 Aug

10.69	7.93	14.69	2.04	47.77	15.28	43.52	4.20	59.80	4:22.80
882	1006	770	891	910	819	754	859	759	639
882	1888	2658	3549	4459	5278	6032	6891	7650	8289

1979

15) **DNF (—)** German Decathlon, Flein, WG 28/29 Jul

10.45	7.60	14.82	2.06	47.30	14.39	43.14	NHC	61.92	withdrawn
946	941	778	909	933	916	746	000	785	
946	1887	2665	3574	4507	5423	6169	6169	6954	

1980

16) **8622* points 1st** International Meeting, Gotzis 17/18 May

10.55	7.72	14.46	2.11	48.04	14.37	42.98	4.90	65.38	4:25.5
919	965	756	950	896	919	743	1028	826	620
919	1884	2640	3590	4486	5405	6148	7176	8002	8622

17) **8495 points 1st** Olympic Games, Moscow 25/26 Jul

10.62	8.00	15.18	2.08	48.01	14.47	42.24	4.70	64.16	4:39.9
900	1020	799	925	898	907	729	981	811	525
900	1920	2719	3644	4542	5449	6178	7159	7970	8495

1981

18) **7936 points 1st** Great Britain-v-Canada, Saskatoon 13/14 Jun

10.47	7.84	14.54	2.05	47.64	14.81w	41.66	5.00	62.54	DNF
940	988	761	900	916	869	718	1052	792	000
940	1928	2689	3589	4505	5374	6092	7144	7936	7936

1982

19) **8704* points 1st** Gotzis International, Gotzis 22/23 May

10.50w	7.95	15.31	2.08	46.86	14.31	44.34	4.90	60.52	4:30.55
932	1010	807	925	955	926	769	1028	767	585
932	1942	2749	3674	4629	5555	6324	7352	8119	8704

20) **8743* points 1st** European Championships, Athens 7/8 Sep

10.51	7.80	15.44	2.03	47.11	14.39	45.48	5.00	63.56	4:23.71
930	980	815	882	942	916	790	1052	804	632
930	1910	2725	3607	4549	5465	6255	7307	8111	8743

21) **8410 points 1st** Commonwealth Games, Brisbane 4/5 Oct

10.66	7.71	15.17	2.04	47.59	15.00	44.58	4.90	62.98	4:43.48
890	963	799	891	918	848	773	1028	797	503
890	1853	2652	3543	4461	5309	6082	7110	7907	8410

1983

22) **8509w points 1st** Canadian Championships, Toronto 7/8 Jun

10.44w	7.63	15.38	2.09	48.73	14.46w	42.20	5.10	62.04	4:42.58
948	947	811	934	863	908	728	1075	786	509
948	1895	2706	3640	4503	5411	6139	7214	8000	8509

23) **8666 points 1st** World Championships, Helsinki 12/13 Aug

10.60	7.88	15.35	2.03	48.12	14.37w	44.46	5.10	65.24	4:29.72
906	996	809	882	893	919	771	1075	824	591
906	1902	2711	3593	4486	5405	6176	7251	8075	8666

*world record. w = wind assisted.

Personal Details

Full name: Francis Morgan Thompson, MBE
Born: Kensington, London, 30.7.58
Height: 1.84m (6'0½")
Weight: 88kg (13st 12lb)

Daley Thompson's Records

World/European
Decathlon: 8622 pts (1980), 8704 (1982), 8743 (1982)

Commonwealth/UK
Decathlon: 7905 pts (1976), 7921 (1977), 8190 (1977), 8238 (1978), 8289 (1978), 8622 (1980), 8704 (1982), 8743 (1982)

World/European Junior
Decathlon: 7905 pts (1976), 7921 (1977), 8190 (1977)

UK Junior
Long jump: 7.49m (1976), 7.57m (1976), 7.72m (1977)
Decathlon: 7100 pts (1975; no application for ratification); 7684 (1976), 7905 (1976), 7921 (1977), 8190 (1977)
4×100m, 2nd leg: 40.74s (1976)

Personal Bests

(w = wind assisted; i = indoors)

60 metres	6.88 i	Crystal Palace	1 Mar 78
100 metres	10.32 w	Crystal Palace	26 Jun 81
	10.36	Pomona, USA	24 Mar 84
200 metres	20.88	Crystal Palace	18 Aug 79
300 metres	33.94	Crystal Palace	31 Jul 81
400 metres	46.86	Gotzis, Austria	22 May 82
600 metres	1:24.4 i	Cosford	19 Jul 77
1000 metres	2:42.19 i	Toronto	12 Feb 84
1500 metres	4:20.3	Cwmbran	23 May 76
60m hurdles	8.06 i	Cosford	26 Jan 80
110m hurdles	14.2	Antrim	26 Jun 82
	14.31	Gotzis, Austria	23 May 82
400m hurdles	52.6	Cwmbran	17 Sep 77
high jump	2.14m i	Amarillo, USA	20 Feb 82
	2.11m	Gotzis, Austria	17 May 80
pole vault	5.20m	Crystal Palace	11 Sep 81
long jump	8.11m w	Edmonton	7 Aug 78
	8.00m	Moscow	26 Jul 80
shot put	16.10m	Walnut, USA	14 Jan 84
discus throw	47.44m	Haringey	22 Aug 81
hammer throw	26.20m	Barking	2 Dec 79
javelin throw	65.38m	Gotzis, Austria	18 May 80
decathlon	8743	Athens	7/8 Sep 82

Olympic Decathlon Champions

1904	(St Louis)	Thomas Kiely (Ireland)	6036
1912	(Stockholm)	*Jim Thorpe (USA)	6756
		*Hugo Wieslander (Swed)	6161
1920	(Antwerp)	Helge Lövland (Norway)	5970
1924	(Paris)	Harold Osborn (USA)	6668
1928	(Amsterdam)	Paavo Yrjölä (Finland)	6774
1932	(Los Angeles)	Jim Bausch (USA)	6896
1936	(Berlin)	Glenn Morris (USA)	7421
1948	(London)	Bob Mathias (USA)	6826
1952	(Helsinki)	Bob Mathias (USA)	7731
1956	(Melbourne)	Milt Campbell (USA)	7708
1960	(Rome)	Rafer Johnson (USA)	8001
1964	(Tokyo)	Willi Holdorf (W.Ger)	7887
1968	(Mexico City)	Bill Toomey (USA)	8193
1972	(Munich)	Nikolai Avilov (USSR)	8454
1976	(Montreal)	Bruce Jenner (USA)	8618
1980	(Moscow)	Daley Thompson (GB)	8495

All scores are based on the current (1962) tables. The 1904 events differed considerably from the standard decathlon events.
*Thorpe finished first in 1912, but was later disqualified for a breach of the amateur rules, and Wieslander placed first; in 1982, the IOC restored Thorpe's gold medal and reinstated him posthumously as joint champion.

Progressive Decathlon World Record

(since 1972)

8454 pts	Nikolai Avilov (USSR)	1972
8524	Bruce Jenner (USA)	1975
8538	Bruce Jenner (USA)	1976
8618	Bruce Jenner (USA)	1976
8622	Daley Thompson (GB)	1980
8649	Guido Kratschmer (WG)	1980
8704	Daley Thompson (GB)	1982
8723	Jurgen Hingsen (WG)	1982
8743	Daley Thompson (GB)	1982
8779	Jurgen Hingsen (WG)	1983

Top Twelve Decathletes 1983

8779	Jurgen Hingsen (WG)
8718	Siegfried Wentz (WG)
8666	Daley Thompson (GB)
8538	Grigoriy Degtyaryov (USSR)
8501	Uwe Freimuth (EG)
8457	Guido Kratschmer (WG)
8418	Konstantin Akhapkin (USSR)
8412	Aleksandr Nevskiy (USSR)
8369	Andreas Rizzi (WG)
8337	Stefan Niklaus (Switz)
8335	Torsten Voss (EG)
8320	Viktor Gruzenkin (USSR)

Progression of Personal Bests

(w = wind assisted; i = indoors; a = automatic timing)

NB Best unassisted and outdoor performances are included even when inferior to wind-assisted and indoor performances.

100 metres (hand timing)

11.9	Eastbourne	30 Jun 73
11.6	Dartford	73
11.2	Dartford	1 Jun 74
11.2		5 Jun 74
11.1	Brighton	22 Jun 74
11.1	Haringey	14 Sep 74
10.9	Barking	19 Apr 75
10.9	Haringey	18 May 75
10.8	Haringey	31 May 75
10.8	C.Palace	17 Aug 75
10.7w	Cwmbran	30 Aug 75
10.8	Cwmbran	22 May 76
10.7	Isleworth	9 Jun 76
10.6	Copenhagen	26 Jun 76
10.6w	Haringey	7 Jul 76
10.5	Talence	4 Sep 76
10.5	Madrid	25 Jun 77
10.4w	Southampton	22 Jun 80
10.5	Leiden	17 Sep 81

100 metres (auto-timing)

10.87	C.Palace	28 Apr 76
10.79	Montreal	29 Jul 76
10.71w	Gotzis	21 May 77
10.71w	C.Palace	18 Jun 77
10.74	C.Palace	18 Jun 77
10.70	Sittard	30 Jul 77
10.68w	C.Palace	3 Jun 78
10.65	Edinburgh	15 Jul 78
10.50w	Edmonton	7 Aug 78
10.63	C.Palace	13 Jul 79
10.56	C.Palace	13 Jul 79
10.49	C.Palace	13 Jul 79
10.45	Flein	28 Jul 79
10.36w	C.Palace	18 Aug 79
10.32w	C.Palace	26 Jun 81
10.36	Pomona, USA	24 Mar 84

200 metres (combined list)

24.1	Eastbourne	30 Jun 73
23.0	Brighton	18 May 74
22.8	Brighton	15 Jun 74
22.4	Brighton	15 Jun 74
22.3	W.London	19 Jul 75
22.0	W.London	19 Jul 75
21.9	Bristol	19 Sep 76
21.8	Cwmbran	12 Jun 77
20.88	C.Palace	18 Aug 79

400 metres (combined list)

56.4	Haywards H.	7 Jul 73
51.5		74
50.8	Haringey	31 May 75
49.9	Luton	8 Jun 75
49.6	Cwmbran	30 Aug 75
49.3	Cwmbran	4 Oct 75
49.03	C.Palace	5 May 76
48.6	Copenhagen	26 Jun 76
48.15	Montreal	29 Jul 76
48.1	Talence	4 Sep 76
48.00	C.Palace	17 Sep 76
47.4	Madrid	25 Jun 77
47.31	Sittard	30 Jul 77
47.30	Flein	28 Jul 79
46.86	Gotzis	22 May 82

1500 metres

4:31.0	Cwmbran	29 Jun 75
4:30.9	Cwmbran	5 Oct 75
4:20.3	Cwmbran	23 May 76

110m hurdles (3′6″; combined list)

21.1	Dartford	1 Jun 74
16.8	Cwmbran	29 Jun 75
15.8w	Cwmbran	31 Aug 75
16.0	Cwmbran	5 Oct 75
15.5	Cwmbran	23 May 76
15.3	Copenhagen	27 Jun 76
15.24	Gotzis	22 May 77
15.1	Madrid	26 Jun 77
14.9w	Edinburgh	2 Jul 77
14.95	Donetsk	20 Aug 77
14.85	Gotzis	28 May 78
14.39	Flein	28 Jul 79
14.37	Gotzis	18 May 80
14.31	Gotzis	23 May 82
14.2	Antrim	26 Jun 82

400m hurdles

52.6	Cwmbran	17 Sep 77

high jump

1.72	Eastbourne	30 Jun 73
1.72	Eastbourne	8 Jul 73
1.80	Brighton	18 May 74
1.93	Brighton	22 Jun 74
1.97	Cwmbran	28 Jun 75
1.98	Woodford	16 Aug 75
1.98	Cwmbran	22 May 76
2.00	Oxford	4 May 77
2.00	Gotzis	21 May 77
2.07	Madrid	25 Jun 77
2.07	Edmonton	7 Aug 78
2.11	Gotzis	17 May 80
2.14 i	Amarillo	20 Feb 82

pole vault

2.44	Barking	10 May 75
2.90	Cwmbran	29 Jun 75
3.30	Cwmbran	31 Aug 75
3.40	Cwmbran	5 Oct 75
3.70 i	Cosford	13 Dec 75
3.70 i	C.Palace	14 Jan 76
3.90 i	C.Palace	11 Feb 76
4.00 i	Cosford	21 Feb 76
4.20	Chiswick	10 Jul 76
4.20	Montreal	30 Jul 76
4.30	C.Palace	22 Aug 76
4.40	Talence	5 Sep 76
4.40 i	Cosford	19 Mar 77
4.40	Chiswick	4 Jun 77
4.50	C.Palace	18 Jun 77
4.80	Madrid	26 Jun 77
4.90	C.Palace	10 Aug 77
4.90	C.Palace	22 Jul 79
5.00	C.Palace	27 Aug 79
5.10	Haringey	30 May 81
5.20	C.Palace	11 Sep 81

long jump

6.48		74
6.99	Cwmbran	28 Jun 75
7.30	Woodford	16 Aug 75
7.40	Cwmbran	22 May 76
7.49	Haringey	13 Jun 76
7.57	Talence	4 Sep 76
7.72	Gotzis	21 May 77
7.95w	Gotzis	27 May 78
7.72w	Southampton	17 Jun 78
8.11w	Edmonton	7 Aug 78
7.93	Prague	30 Aug 78
8.00	Moscow	26 Jul 80

shot put

7.00	Eastbourne	30 Jun 73
10.80	Barking	10 May 75
10.95	Chiswick	21 Jun 75
11.77	Cwmbran	4 Oct 75
12.95	Cosford (i)	13 Dec 75
12.79	Cwmbran	22 May 76
12.85	Haringey	7 Jul 76
13.10	Montreal	29 Jul 76
13.59	Talence	4 Sep 76
13.65	C.Palace (i)	8 Jan 77
14.32	Cosford (i)	19 Mar 77
14.09	Haringey	10 Apr 77
14.53	Birmingham	20 May 78
14.69	Prague	30 Aug 78
14.82	Flein	28 Jul 79
15.09	Cosford (i)	7 Nov 79
15.24	Cosford (i)	7 Nov 79
15.45	Cosford (i)	7 Nov 79
15.03	C.Palace	6 May 81
15.32	Leicester	16 Aug 81
15.44	Athens	7 Sep 82
16.10	Walnut	14 Jan 84

Discus throw (2kg)

31.42	Cwmbran	28 Jun 75
32.20	Cwmbran	31 Aug 75
40.22	Haringey	9 May 76
41.80	Woodford	23 Apr 77
42.78	Woodford	11 Sep 77
44.46	Barking	18 Jul 78
45.22	C.Palace	1 Aug 79
46.64	Barking	8 Jun 80
47.44	Haringey	22 Aug 81

javelin throw (800g)

44.46	Haringey (700g)	14 Sep 74
47.12	Chiswick	21 Jun 75
51.88	Cwmbran	29 Jun 75
53.28	Cwmbran	31 Aug 75
57.04	Cwmbran	5 Oct 75
59.02	Birmingham	20 May 78
59.42	Haringey	25 Jun 78
59.80	Prague	31 Aug 78
59.86	Stretford	5 May 79
60.76	W.London	26 May 79
61.92	Flein	29 Jul 79
62.00	C.Palace	27 Aug 79
62.34	Wolverhampton	3 May 80
65.38	Gotzis	18 May 80

Selection from current decathlon scoring tables (compiled 1962, revised 1971, 1977)

Points	100m	long jump	shot put	high jump	400m	110m hurdles	discus throw	pole vault	javelin throw	1500m
1	15.6s	3.60m	4.71m	1.14m	78.05s	31.9 s	12.82m	1.50m	14.03m	6:39.6
500	12.40	5.54	10.55	1.61	57.90	19.18	31.14	2.91	40.59	4:44.0
550	12.15	5.76	11.27	1.66	56.44	18.45	33.42	3.08	44.00	4:36.0
600	11.90	5.98	12.01	1.72	55.05	17.76	35.77	3.25	47.56	4:28.4
650	11.67	6.21	12.77	1.77	53.73	17.13	38.20	3.42	51.25	4:21.3
700	11.44	6.44	13.55	1.83	52.47	16.54	40.72	3.60	55.09	4:14.5
725	11.33	6.55	13.95	1.85	51.86	16.26	42.01	3.69	57.06	4:11.3
750	11.22	6.67	14.36	1.88	51.27	15.99	43.31	3.79	59.06	4:08.2
775	11.12	6.79	14.77	1.91	50.69	15.72	44.64	3.88	61.10	4:05.0
800	11.01	6.90	15.19	1.94	50.12	15.47	45.99	3.98	63.17	4:02.0
825	10.91	7.03	15.62	1.97	49.57	15.22	47.35	4.07	65.27	3:59.0
850	10.81	7.15	16.05	2.00	49.02	14.99	48.75	4.17	67.42	3:56.1
875	10.71	7.27	16.48	2.03	48.49	14.75	50.16	4.27	69.60	3:53.4
900	10.62	7.40	16.92	2.05	47.97	14.53	51.58	4.37	71.81	3:50.6
925	10.52	7.52	17.37	2.08	47.46	14.31	53.03	4.47	74.05	3:47.9
950	10.43	7.65	17.82	2.11	46.97	14.10	54.50	4.57	76.33	3:45.3
975	10.34	7.78	18.28	2.14	46.48	13.90	55.99	4.68	78.64	3:42.7
1000	10.25	7.90	18.75	2.17	46.00	13.70	57.50	4.78	81.00	3:40.2
1025	10.16	8.03	19.22	2.20	45.53	13.51	59.02	4.89	83.38	3:37.7
1050	10.08	8.16	19.69	2.23	45.07	13.32	60.57	4.99	85.80	3:35.3
1075	9.99	8.29	20.18	2.27	44.62	13.14	62.14	5.10	88.26	3:33.0
1100	9.91	8.42	20.66	2.30	44.18	12.96	63.73	5.21	90.74	3:30.7
1200	9.58	8.96	22.68	2.40+	42.51	12.29	70.29	5.66	101.03	3:22.0

NB In cases where the exact number of points in the left-hand column is not awarded, the next best time, distance, or height is given.